Project Neptune

A Suspense Thriller

By

Thomas Velsun

About the Author:

Thomas Velsun lives with his wife in coastal Florida. He's a former Army officer and a veteran of the Vietnam War. After leaving the Military he spent forty years in business and retired from a large global technology company.

The knowledge gained from his three college degrees from three different major universities (a BS in Math and Accounting, an MS in Engineering, and an MBA) has contributed heavily to his success in business and to his grasp of the subject matter in his novels.

During his business career, he completed special projects with various government agencies in Washington DC, including the FBI,CIA,US Mint, and IRS. He has participated in special projects with RAND Corporation (a think tank formed after World War II to continue the activities of various experts accumulated during the war years). He has worked in many different areas in the United States and in foreign countries. He has researched many conspiracy theories and has included selected subject matter from some of them in his novels.

He's a former athlete and maintains fitness with daily workouts involving weightlifting. He also enjoys playing golf and tennis.

Chapter 1

The intelligence data verifying the Russian Oligarchs Ivan Titov and Sergei Nikitin were still active dominated Colt Randall's thoughts as he walked toward the double doors composed of bulletproof glass guarding the front entrance of Boswic Corporation (Boswic) in Tampa, Florida.

Four steel posts were spread three feet apart and were anchored in concrete six feet in front of the doors. These latest security precautions were installed last week.

Colt punched in the security code and entered the building. Within five minutes he sat with three other people at a small round conference table in his boss's office.

Jim Boxer, Colt's boss and Vice President at Boswic, scanned the faces around the table as he prepared to start the scheduled meeting to discuss the current threat situation. Linda Martinez, Colt's partner, and Blake Morgan, Boswic's top tactics analyst, also sat at the table.

After looking directly at Colt, Jim said, "Since Titov

and Nikitin escaped from the action in Jamaica, they've probably returned to their base close to Finland. They'll try to retaliate for sure, and you can expect to have a big target on your back."

"That's no surprise," Colt replied. "And I'm certain the Kremlin will again supply them with everything they need."

Jim nodded and then looked at Linda. "I expect there will be a target on your back too."

Linda grunted. "They'll want revenge, but Colt will probably be the one they concentrate on."

"We'll all need to stay on our toes," Jim said. "They might even try launching more Poseidon Missiles. The ones China enhanced with the new steering mechanism driven by a quantum computer can easily reach us from Finland."

Blake scanned the faces around the table. "Titov and Nikitin will probably have a large supply to draw from and it's likely they'll use some of them."

"Do you think the Chinese enhanced some other aspects of the missiles too?" Linda asked.

"The best data we've collected indicates the missiles normally travel underwater at a speed of 80 miles an hour," Blake said. "That's faster than our nuclear-powered attack submarines and it's also faster than our sub's anti-ship missiles. The Poseidon Missiles can also travel at a depth of 3,280 feet. That's far lower than any of our submarines can go."

"Remember, the Russians call it their Tsunami Apocalypse Torpedo," Jim replied. "Since it's powered by a miniature nuclear reactor, it effectively has unlimited range. That's another reason it can hit us from Finland."

"There's another thing we should mention," Blake said. "We've now confirmed the Chinese have helped Russia improve the speed to exceed 200 miles per hour. They have added ramjet engines and have been able to create a bubble of gas for the missile to travel in. This reduces friction with the water."

Jim shook his head slowly. "The possibility of the Russians hitting us from Finland is certainly very much in play."

Colt looked directly at Jim. "Do you think China will continue to partner with Russia on this?"

"I think that's likely," Jim said. "They both want to bring us down so they can dominate the world."

Colt gave a short laugh. "I don't think they can both dominate at the same time. If they succeed in bringing us down, they'll be in competition for who will be the world leader."

"Yeah, they'll be fighting each other, but that won't matter to us if we've already been defeated," Blake said.

A brief silence ensued.

Jim narrowed his eyes. "We'll move over to our main conference room and continue this discussion with Harlan. We must make sure we keep succeeding in helping to defend the United States of America."

Chapter 2

At a secure base on an unnamed island just off the western shore of Finland, two determined individuals again prepared to launch a lethal attack on the United States. This time they planned to work harder and smarter to ensure it would succeed.

Ivan Titov looked across a small round conference table in his office at his partner, Sergei Nikitin.

"The Kremlin wants revenge and they want it with an exclamation point added," Ivan said. "They want the ultimate revenge. They want to kill Colt Randall and also destroy a major area in the United States of America at the same time. They want revenge with impact, maximum impact."

"Does the Kremlin want to make a clear statement to the rest of the world they won't be pushed around, especially by an individual named Colt Randall?" Sergei asked.

Ivan nodded. "And they still want to maintain some level of deniability even though they're aware United States intelligence agencies know the Kremlin is behind what's been going on."

"What good does maintaining deniability do them?"

Ivan shrugged. "I think they feel it's a cushion to avoid an all-out war. If they don't get directly involved in our activity they can declare we went rogue and followed our own agenda."

"We want to destroy a major area in the United States and then take over what the Americans have left. Why doesn't the Kremlin put their full effort into doing that? Why not have an all-out war?"

"I doubt the Kremlin thinks they can win."

"What if China helps us?"

"I'm told that could end up being complicated. China will want to control everything. The Kremlin wants to be in charge, and they don't want to fight China to do that."

Sergei nodded slowly.

There was a brief silence.

"Well, that was definitely a setback in Jamaica, but we survived and here we are with another chance to bring the United States down," Ivan said. "We can't really complain about our situation."

"Do you know what we're going to do this time?"

"We have two Poseidon Missiles being shipped to us from China. Each one is 80 feet long and 8 feet wide and each one of them carries a 100-megaton warhead."

Sergei leaned forward. "You're referring to the missiles China was in the process of upgrading when we were in Jamaica?"

Ivan nodded. "The Chinese technicians have finished retrofitting them to carry the larger warhead. And, like I told you, they're both on their way to us."

"Who in the Kremlin is keeping you informed?"

"Our new bosses, Lev Petrov and Yuri Werner," Ivan said. He gave a slight grin. "They called me about thirty minutes ago."

Sergei narrowed his eyes. "Why didn't you tell me?"

"I'm telling you now. I wanted to check a few things

first."

"What things?"

"Odds and ends," Ivan said. "I didn't find any information of any significance." He gave a slight shrug. "Don't worry about it. Let's get back to the main discussion. I have a lot more to tell you."

Sergei didn't comment.

"Our new bosses are coming here tomorrow. We'll both get a chance to meet them and get some questions answered."

"What else do you have to tell me?"

"I'm getting to that. Have a little patience," Ivan said. "Do you have any more questions about the missiles before I go to the next subject?"

"How are they being shipped?"

"Lev mentioned we should find out real soon. He's waiting to get more details."

Sergei narrowed his eyes. "You didn't press him hard for an immediate answer?"

"I figured that might not be the best thing to do with either of our new bosses. We need to get to know them better before we start doing things like that, besides, he might not know."

"Did Lev mention anything about when we can expect the missiles to arrive?"

"He told me the arrival date isn't definite yet. He thinks he'll find out when he gets the details on the method of shipping. He told me he thought both missiles would arrive soon, definitely within a few days."

"How much do you know about our new bosses?"

"Just a little," Ivan said. "That's what I was taking a little time to research."

Sergei leaned forward, elbows on table, and asked, "Well, what do you know?"

"They've both been in the Russian Navy for thirty years," Ivan said. "They've each been promoted to Admiral and they're going to spend full time advising us on this new project the Kremlin has named Project Neptune."

Sergei gave a short laugh. "You'd think they could come with something a little more original this time."

"Yeah," Ivan said. "I made a few comments about that."

"What did Lev say?"

"He told me that we're going to do basically the same things as we had planned before, but now we're going to do them from a different location and with more support. He emphasized this time we need to make damned sure everything goes as planned and he and Yuri will help on that."

"We just have two missiles, but they're newer and larger missiles and they have a lot more firepower." Sergei leaned forward. "It's good each one has a100 megaton warhead."

Ivan nodded. "Lev mentioned that and he also mentioned a lot of other differences from The Poseidon Initiative." Ivan went on to explain.

"But we still have the same goals as last time?"

"That's right," Ivan said. "Lev told me they were originally going to name this next initiative The Poseidon Initiative II, but they collectively thought that might hamper communications. The decision group didn't want any confusion going forward."

"Did Lev tell you who was in the decision group?"

"No but he mentioned they want to do things differently. This time they want to reach all our goals."

Sergei narrowed his eyes. "We definitely need to succeed if we want to have any future in Russia."

Ivan held his right fist in the air. "This time you and I will work smarter and harder to reach our goals."

Sergei also raised his right fist. "And it sounds like we'll get better support this time."

Chapter 3

In the main conference room at Boswic in Tampa, Colt Randall leaned back in his chair at the large conference table and prepared for more discussion of the looming threats they all faced, threats on the whole United States of America.

Harlan Pierce, the Executive Director of Boswic, scanned the faces around the large table.

Along with Colt, Jim, Linda, and Blake sat at the table with Harlan.

"We'll probably see more activity from Ivan Titov and Sergei Nikitin soon," Harlan said. "I'm guessing the Kremlin wants revenge for what just happened in Jamaica." He looked at Colt. "You were the main thorn in their side. They'll probably come directly after you in some way."

"I'll stay alert," Colt said. "I'm sure we'll all stay alert." Colt expected some more big global events real soon and he was reasonably certain Boswic would be right in the middle of the activity.

"Our intelligence agencies have been busy, and it looks

like we have an expanded threat-matrix this time," Harlan said. He looked at a sheet of paper in front of him and started reading. "An elite cabal of wealthy individuals has been called the Establishment, the Invisible Government, the Illuminati, the Secret Brotherhood, the Power Elite, and several other things. These could be separate organizations, interrelated, or all one and the same." He gestured toward Blake. "Give us a brief review on what we discussed and then let's hear your opinion on the latest twists we might have to deal with."

"We already know there's a powerful covert influence involved in many of our government decisions. Many global societies conduct activity utilizing secret power structures," Blake said. "One society in particular is heavily involved in some new Russian activity."

Colt noted Blake clinched his right fist as he talked.

"How did you get your latest information?" Jim asked.

"I've received a lot of updated intelligence reports from several agencies, I've studied every report closely, and I've discussed all of my conclusions with Steve and Nick," Blake said. "When they both agree with any of my conclusions, we always spend a lot of time digging deeper into the related data."

Colt knew Blake was referring to Steve Lockett, FBI technology specialist, and Nick Wallace, CIA technology specialist. Blake had worked closely with both of them on analytical and technical matters over the last couple of years.

"Don't forget the review," Harlan said. "Some of us need to refresh our knowledge on the relevant history involved in this situation."

Blake studied the people sitting around the table. "We'll start with the Knights Templar who raided Solomon's Temple and absconded with great wealth. Long story short, they eventually hooked up with the Free Masons and the inner core of that group evolved into the

Illuminati."

Everyone remained silent.

"Over the last few years, I've completed extensive research on the Illuminati," Blake said. "They're a well-organized group of Power Elite. They're referenced by a lot of different names, and they're sometimes referred to as the Establishment."

"Does that relate to our current concern about new threats?" Linda asked.

"Some of the secret societies are currently major operatives for the Establishment," Blake said. "They've expanded their reach into Russia. Both Ivan Titov and Sergei Nikitin are involved in the current conspiracy. A couple of new names have been picked up from some calls NSA recently intercepted, Lev Petrov and Yuri Werner." Blake looked around the table. "Based on what has been decrypted from the calls, they're going to be working closely with Titov and Nikitin to plan a new attack on the United States."

Jim grunted. "Well, we've been expecting something like this."

Everyone nodded.

Harlan made an impatient gesture toward Blake. "Keep going."

"One Society has an annual, unofficial, invitation-only conference of around 150 people from North America and Western Europe. About a third of them are from government and the rest are from finance, industry, and education," Blake said. "All, of course, are people of influence. This time some Russians and some Chinese will be involved."

"What subjects will this next meeting include?" Harlan asked.

"This next meeting will have a broader scope," Blake said. "They'll discuss major problems facing the World and then come up with some type of action plan. This time the action plan will probably include some type of retaliation against the United States for what happened in Jamaica."

Harlan narrowed his eyes. "That would be logical if Russians and Chinese are both involved."

Colt looked directly at Blake. "Do you have any specifics about any action plans they have?"

"Not yet," Blake said. "A lot of content from the phone calls hasn't been decrypted. We should get more information later."

Harlan's gaze took in both Colt and Linda. "I'm sure you both have targets on your backs. You need to be real careful as we go forward."

"We shouldn't wait around and try to play defense," Colt said. "I think Linda and I will be a lot more comfortable if we go on the offensive immediately."

Linda nodded. "We know enough to raid their island base off the shore of Finland."

"Grant told me they're trying to work it out as soon as possible," Harlan said. "Our government will need to work with the Government of Finland and probably the Government of Sweden too on this before we launch an attack." He reached for his phone. "I need to call Grant and set up a meeting for all of us over in his office. We'll get his latest input from the various intelligence agencies and then continue our discussion."

Colt felt more optimism than anxiety. He was ready to get started on whatever preparations they needed to make.

Chapter 4

On his island base off the west coast of Finland, Ivan sat in his office and looked across his desk at Sergei. "Are you ready to meet our new bosses?"

"Ready as I'll ever be."

Ivan leaned forward. "I found out earlier today our old bosses were executed."

Sergei asked, "For our failure in Jamaica?"

"That's what Lev told me."

"Who did it?"

"Lev wasn't sure, but he thinks it was some of our President's security force."

There was a brief silence.

"Do you think they'll come after us?" Sergei asked.

"Lev thinks we'll be given another chance since we're well positioned to launch the next attack."

"We lost all three of our top assassins. We also lost our top expert on international banking, along with one of our top experts on computers," Sergei said. "Are we going to get some new help?"

"I hope so. I'm sure Lev and Yuri will discuss that when they get here."

Sergei slowly rubbed his chin and didn't comment.

"We still have our moles in the United States Government," Ivan said. "I'm sure they'll continue to be a big help."

"They all still have close connections to China, right?"

Ivan nodded slowly. "That's my understanding."

"You told me the Kremlin probably doesn't want to stay closely connected with China, right?"

"They might find it beneficial to maintain some type of relationship." Ivan narrowed his eyes. "I'm confident the Kremlin will let us know what they want us to do after they decide how they want to progress. I know they're still discussing things with China. They each want to bring down the United States, and our continued cooperation could be very valuable to both countries."

"China likely has many replicas of our biggest Poseidon Missile in their arsenal now."

Ivan narrowed his eyes. "That was something we knew would happen, but our gain has been more than our loss. China contributed enough technology to give us a much more advanced missile to keep in our arsenal for future use. Even if they do have their own versions of our Poseidon Missiles. They won't use them against us."

"Are you sure about that?"

Ivan narrowed his eyes. "We've talked about this before. We'll leave dealing with all that up to the Kremlin. The Kremlin will have to figure out all the angles and keep us advised."

"Are they working on that?"

"I'm sure they are," Ivan said, "we'll see what Lev and Yuri have to say."

Sergei nodded slowly.

"We'll concentrate on bringing down the United States and then I'm sure the Kremlin will have a way to keep

China from attacking us and taking us over."

"Did Lev mention anything about what our initial strategy is going to be?" Sergei asked.

"He told me we'll ease into things a little more this time," Ivan said. "He emphasized it would be foolish to rush and make a big mistake. This time we all know we must succeed."

Chapter 5

In the main conference room at the FBI Office in Tampa, Colt, Linda, Blake, Harlan and Jim occupied the large table along with Grant Winston, the FBI Special Agent in Charge (SAC).

"Those of us here in Tampa need to coordinate closely," Grant said. "I'm also working closely with our office in Washington and with all the other intelligence agencies. NSA has intercepted more phone calls from the islands off the west cost of Finland into the Washington area. NSA has decrypted various words here and there and we've picked up several names."

Harlan leaned forward. "Probably Ivan Titov and Sergei Nikitin are two of them, right?"

"Right," Grant said. "And NSA has picked up a couple more. Lev Petrov and Yuri Werner have also been mentioned."

"Do we know anything about the new people?" Colt asked.

"They're both high-ranking admirals in the Russian

Navy," Grant said. "And it looks like they're planning something big. There are a lot of communications with a lot of different people involved."

"Are they planning to launch more damn Poseidon Missiles?" Harlan asked.

"That was mentioned," Grant said. "No surprise, they're planning on launching them from Finland." He looked at Colt and Linda. "And also no surprise, you were both mentioned in several of the conversations."

"We'll plan to stay alert," Colt said. He glanced at Linda.

Linda nodded. "We know what we're up against."

Colt noted she didn't seem overly concerned. He already knew she had a lot of courage.

"It's obvious Russia and China are still cooperating with each other. I guess they still want to put their best effort into bringing us down without starting another world war," Grant said. "And there's something else of real interest. Titov and Nikitin have a supercomputer at their base."

Jim leaned forward. "Is it going to be used for hacking?"

"Maybe," Grant said. "There are some things we need to figure out. This whole puzzle fits neatly into the reasons we have Boswic under contract."

Jim narrowed his eyes. "Exactly what do you expect us to do this time?"

"The same things you've done before," Grant said. "Along with providing some expert firepower to help us deal with the pending threats, help us root out some active elements of various secret societies involved in the threats. We know both Russia and China are working closely with the Illuminati. Like he's done before, Blake should be able to provide some excellent help on various types of analysis."

Harlan nodded slowly.

Jim leaned toward Grant. "Do you think this secret society stuff might be the stimulus behind Russia and China wanting to control the world?"

"Our staff in Washington thinks there's a connection," Grant said. "I hope you'll allow Blake to continue to do a lot of consulting with Steve."

Harlan grunted and looked at Blake. "We'll need a quick start on putting the new pieces of this puzzle together. Plan to spend a lot of time on it."

Blake gave a thumbs-up and nodded.

"It looks like our gold supply is involved in this again," Grant said. He looked at Blake. "Plan to do more analysis in that area."

"We think the Federal Reserve Bank of New York has the biggest gold supply in the world," Blake replied. "However, we don't own much of it."

Colt nodded. "I understand foreign investors own most of it."

"That's correct," Blake said. "The U.S. can only claim about 5% of it. There are 5,000 metric tons of gold in the vault in New York. That's supposed to be 500 metric tons more than Fort Knox. At least we own what's in Fort Knox."

"Are you trying to make any particular point?" Jim asked.

"Not really," Blake said, "just trying to refresh everyone's memory and provide some perspective relating to the gold supply," he looked at Grant, "since you mentioned that was part of this current situation we're dealing with."

There was a brief silence.

Harlan looked at Grant. "Have we been getting any direct help from NRO on scouting the situation on the islands off the shore of Finland?" Harlan asked.

Colt knew the NRO (National Reconnaissance Office) designed, built, and operated the reconnaissance satellites of the United States government. An agency in the Department of Defense, it coordinated collection and analysis of information from both airplane and satellite reconnaissance by the military services and the CIA. The FBI was a primary recipient of data from locations they requested.

"Quite a bit," Grant said. "I won't go into all the details right now, but we should have a lot of new information real soon."

Harlan gave a slow nod.

"We know Titov and Nikitin are both billionaires and we know they're smart," Grant said. "We know they work for the Kremlin and China is directly involved, but we now know there's a higher intellectual layer involved in what they're doing, probably the Illuminati are involved. We're convinced something real big is going on again and it likely involves launching Poseidon Missiles toward our shores."

Harlan grunted and drummed his fingers on the table for a moment. "This whole thing is going to be one gigantic challenge, even bigger than before."

Grant nodded. "It's shaping up to be the most complex puzzle I've ever been involved with."

Jim rubbed his chin and appeared thoughtful. "If we don't stop this thing pretty soon, we'll have an even bigger problem."

Harlan nodded. "We need to figure out what's connected and what's not. This is going to take all the resources we have available and we all need to work closely together to make fast progress."

Knowing some timely action would again be necessary Colt figured a trip to the islands off the western shore of Finland would be necessary real soon. He was confident he and Linda would be part of the ensuing taskforce.

Chapter 6

In the main conference room on his island base off the west coast of Finland, Ivan and Sergei looked across the large table at Lev and Yuri.

"You'll soon receive the two newest Poseidon Missiles from China, and you'll launch them from here," Lev said. "We'll get our revenge and throw in an extra powerful punch too. Everything has been approved by the Kremlin."

"Have our targets been defined?" Ivan asked.

"We want to demonstrate to the Americans how destructive we can be when we choose to attack them and both missiles will be exploded in the Tampa area," Lev said. "Our experts are still working on the exact coordinates for each missile to hit."

Yuri nodded. "We'll take out Colt Randall, Boswic Corporation, Tampa, Saint Petersburg, and MacDill Air Force Base all at the same time."

"The explosions will also take out a lot more strategic

assets the Americans have in that area," Lev said. "Our experts are still working on clarifying every detail."

"How will we make sure Randall is there when we strike?" Ivan asked.

"Remember, we have a lot of capability for control of these missiles," Yuri said. "We'll get the missiles into their positions and then we'll wait to detonate them until we've confirmed Randall's location."

Both Ivan and Sergei remained silent. Ivan figured an explanation would follow quickly.

"We'll use several of our satellites to do the necessary surveillance," Yuri said. "The 100 megatons of explosive power in each missile will be detonated after we've confirmed Randall will be in the blast area."

Lev narrowed his eyes. "Remember the Poseidon Missile can travel at a depth of 3,280 feet. We'll work out the details later as to where we position them while we're ensuring Randall is there."

Yuri nodded. "We don't want them to be detected, and we might end up keeping them further out in the Gulf in deeper water. We'll make a decision on that after all the details are worked out."

There was a brief silence.

"So, what's our next step here?" Ivan asked.

Lev leaned forward and put his elbows on the table. "We'll discuss the preparations later that you need to make here." He gestured toward Yuri. "We'll go over all the details and provide any necessary clarifications to help you move things along as fast as you can."

"Do we have an actual arrival date yet for the missiles?" Ivan asked.

"They were shipped from Beijing to a place along the China coastline two days ago but there are still some remaining steps in the process of shipping them here," Lev said. "We don't want our enemies to discover they're coming here, so we have a lot of decoys involved. We're trying to make it impossible for anyone to even discover the missiles are being moved."

"How will we launch them from here?" Sergei asked.

"We'll probably build a launch site of some sort close to this location," Yuri said. "We aren't sure yet how sophisticated it will need to be. The design will probably depend on how other things progress."

"Are Sergei and I in charge of the final preparations for the launch like we were before?" Ivan asked.

"We see how that evolves." Lev narrowed his eyes and glanced at Ivan.

Ivan gave a slow nod.

Sergei didn't comment.

"None of us will make any decisions about exactly when we're going to strike our target," Lev said. "Those decisions will be made higher up in the Kremlin."

"Will China have any participation in making any decisions this time?" Sergei asked.

"I don't know," Lev said, "I was told there's always that possibility. We'll have to see how things develop."

"So, we're just going to carry out our orders from the Kremlin when we receive them?" Ivan asked.

"You'll receive all your orders from Yuri and me," Lev said. "We're going to constantly receive a lot of intelligence, and we'll stay in close communication with our boss at the Kremlin."

"Will Sergei and I constantly discuss all the relevant details with the two of you as we move forward?" Ivan asked.

"Yes and those details will probably be constantly changing," Lev said. "As before, you and Sergei will be responsible for all the tactical decisions. You'll be expected to make the necessary adjustments and execute properly when you receive specific orders from Yuri and me."

Ivan and Sergei both nodded slowly.

"There will be a large number of people in Moscow

who will be constantly working to make sure we're provided all the resources we'll need," Yuri said. "Even though the top decision makers in the Kremlin want to stay in the background, we'll still get all the necessary support."

There was a brief silence.

"It's going to be interesting to see what decisions are made on selecting the exact coordinates for the missiles to hit." Ivan took a deep breath, exhaled slowly, and leaned back in his chair. "There's quite a difference in the impact of a 100-megaton warhead and a 2-megaton warhead."

"We won't have to worry about any of those details," Lev said. "The four of us just have to follow instructions from our top decision makers and make sure the missiles get launched on time."

Sergei narrowed his eyes. "I'm guessing China will continue to have a large influence on most decisions the Kremlin makes in this regard."

Lev and Yuri both hesitated for a few moments and then each of them nodded slowly.

"China has continued to pour a lot of money into our efforts against the United States," Lev said. "They have mostly the same interests."

Ivan mulled over the situation and glanced at Sergei. There was a lot to think about.

Sergei showed no reaction and made no comment.

"Well, I guess we've covered enough for now," Lev said. "We'll stay in close touch." He and Yuri both stood and made their exit.

Chapter 7

Colt sat beside Linda in a conference room at Boswic. They both looked across the large table at Blake.

"Jim told me NSA has intercepted more phone calls and more funding for launching Poseidon Missiles has been discussed." Colt looked directly at Blake. "He suggested Linda and I have another discussion with you on the financial aspects of what Russia and China will probably want to do."

Blake nodded. "Yeah, he thinks it's good for both of you to have a better understanding of the whole scope of what you're going to be coping with."

"Colt and I have read your paper several times where you covered multiple aspects of global financing," Linda said. "We need to stay updated on your thinking in that regard. The extra knowledge could come in handy in certain situations."

"I know the FBI has teamed with the CIA to beef up security at the World Bank," Blake replied. "The FBI is concentrating on the domestic considerations. The CIA has been looking into all the international aspects. It still appears the main pipeline for funding any big project for launching Poseidon Missiles is going through the World Bank via the IMF."

Colt narrowed his eyes. "Review the basic details for us again."

Blake leaned forward. "Speaking globally, the most prominent international financial institutions are the IMF, the World Bank, and the WTO."

"And the WTO is the World Trade Organization?" Colt asked.

Blake nodded. "They negotiate international trade agreements and settle trade disputes. Money, of course, is always involved. That's one way they get into the mix of international financing. The World Bank and the IMF do their things, and the details are really complicated."

"And you've told us before the World Bank has a lot of different components, right?" Linda asked.

"Yes," Blake said. "That's one way this gets complicated. It's often referenced as the World Bank Group. It's composed of five different international organizations. They're normally referred to as IBRD, IDA, IFC, MIGA, and ICSID. They all play a part in this."

"And you mentioned before some of the global money flow has a connection to our Federal Reserve System, right?" Colt asked.

Blake nodded. "There's a reason why the money is in United States dollars." He went on to give more details.

Linda stared at Blake. "Would you refresh our memories on the names for those five agencies in the World Bank system?"

"IBRD stands for International Bank for Reconstruction and Development. IDA stands for

International Development Association," Blake said. "Actually, when someone is referring to the World Bank, they're generally referring to those two agencies."

Linda and Colt both nodded.

"IFC stands for International Finance Corporation," Blake said, "MIGA stands for Multilateral Investment Guarantee Agency, and ICSID stands for International Centre for Settlement of Investment Disputes."

"Using multiple entities could create a lot of confusion about the source of any funds," Colt replied. "And that's what the Russians and Chinese always want to do if they don't want to be identified."

Blake nodded and then said, "The Federal Reserve Bank of Chicago has an international finance conference every year. They invite researchers and policymakers from a lot of different countries." He looked directly at Colt. "The World Bank Group provides financial assets and advice to countries for the purposes of economic development and eliminating poverty. A few insiders can throw a good smoke screen over the financing for specific activities."

There was a brief silence.

"Getting on to another aspect of this," Blake said. "Both a quantum computer and a supercomputer were mentioned in some of the intercepted calls. They'll be used by Russia and China to move the money around on a new joint project they're planning. Do you want to hear the details about the computers again?"

"Go on and tell us" Colt said. "We could use a little more insight into the technical details involved in this. Nick will probably refer to some of them in his future briefings to us. He always does that. It will be a good thing if we understand more of what he tells us without having to ask a lot of questions."

"The Russians will be getting another Chinese supercomputer, a Sunway Taihulight. Remember this computer is based on a Field-Programmable Gate Array," Blake said. "The technology is commonly referenced as FPGA."

"Now what's the speed of this supercomputer?" Linda narrowed her eyes and stared at Blake.

Blake smiled. "Do you remember what a FLOP is?"

"It wouldn't hurt to go over it again," Colt said. "We don't work with all that stuff everyday like you do."

"FLOP stands for floating point operation," Blake replied. "FLOPS are how many per second. Our primary measure of speed right now is in Petaflops. That's a thousand trillion FLOPS. Or a quadrillion FLOPS. You could also say a thousand teraflops. The latest Chinese supercomputers have achieved a speed of 2.57 Petaflops."

Colt and Linda both pursed their lips and nodded.

"Regarding the quantum computer, NMR is the most common component in the architecture," Blake said. "That's Nuclear magnetic resonance and it makes it a billion times faster than the best conventional computer and a lot faster than the Chinese supercomputer."

"When you briefed us on this before, I think you told us the quantum computer operates on the Superposition Principle," Colt said.

Blake nodded. "That relates to atoms being in several different energy states at once. Meaning it can act on all variable states simultaneously, carrying out numerous computations in parallel. That gives it tremendous speed. It uses molecules that interact with one another as qubits. Each molecule consists of the nuclei from five fluorine and two carbon atoms."

Colt gave a short laugh and glanced at Linda. "I guess we can consider ourselves to be updated on the latest aspects involving finance and fast computers."

"And it looks like that might have some relevance to our upcoming mission," Linda said.

Colt exhaled slowly. "Yeah, and we probably know as

much about the technical aspects of all that as we want to right now."

"I can agree with Colt's statement," Linda said. "My brain is about saturated with all the details." She looked at Blake and gave a slight grin.

Colt said, "Linda and I appreciate the information. It could be useful to be more aware of the different aspects we'll probably have to deal with." He glanced again at Linda. "Both the financial aspects and the computer aspects are certainly part of the picture we're dealing with."

Linda gave a slow nod.

"One thing we've learned from the intercepted phone calls is that we're going to be facing some new threats," Blake said. "It looks like we'll again need to put forth our best effort to succeed in preventing a catastrophe for our country."

Knowing Blake's statement was true, Colt felt determination swell within him. He would do all he could to eliminate this latest threat to the continued existence of the United States.

Blake's gaze took in both Colt and Linda. "Do either of you have any more questions at this time?"

"Have you talked to Nick or Steve this morning?" Colt asked.

"I talked to both of them right before this meeting," Blake said. "I wanted to make sure I had all the latest information they had before I talked to you."

"Did each of them have the same information?" Linda asked.

"All three of us had exactly the same details," Blake said. "The FBI, the CIA, and Boswic are closely coordinated and we three analysts intend to keep it that way to the best of our ability."

There was a brief silence.

Colt knew close cooperation was essential and he hoped CIA field agent, Mack Thompson, got assigned to work with him and Linda again. The three of them made a good team.

"Any more questions?" Blake asked.

Colt glanced at Linda and then looked back toward Blake.

"I think we're as up to date as we need to be," Colt said. He figured coordination was going to be a critical element for their success in going forward. He hoped Harlan, Charles Andrews, the CIA Director, and Ken Johnson, the FBI Director all would facilitate working closely together as much as they could.

Blake stood, as did Colt and Linda. They all moved toward the door.

Chapter 8

At CIA Headquarters in McLean, Virginia, Charles Andrews (the CIA Director) sat at the round conference table in his office and met with some of his key agents.

Paul Collins (head of the Terrorist Threat Investigation Unit at the CIA), Nick Wallace (a CIA technology specialist reporting to Paul Collins), and Mack Thomson (the top CIA field agent) all waited for Charles to start the meeting.

Charles looked at Nick. "Have you had some conversations with Blake Morgan down at Boswic?"

"A lot," Nick said, "three times today already."

Charles nodded slowly. "I have a conversation with Ken Johnson over at the FBI at least twice a day. He assures me they're fully prepared to continue to work closely with us. He also assures me he stays in close contact with Harlan Pierce at Boswic, and they're all ready to move forward on forming the new taskforce."

"I'll get that discussion started," Paul said. "Nick and I have all the relevant aspects fully analyzed."

Charles gave a slow nod. "I know the President wants to get all the latest intelligence information before we put the finishing touches on our plan. NRO has a lot of surveillance satellites focused on the area off the western shore of Finland, and NSA is trying to pick up more relevant phone conversations. We'll make sure we know what we're doing before we go over there."

"While we're waiting for the latest details, do you have any new information we can discuss relative to those islands?" Paul asked.

Charles pointed toward a scene displayed on a wall monitor in his office. "It looks certain the archipelago of tiny islands between Finland and Sweden is going to be our target. We need to do some more analysis and get much more specific. There are a lot of islands in that archipelago, and we need to know exactly which ones will be our main targets."

"Any idea how many islands are involved in this threat right now?" Paul gestured toward the monitor.

"No," Charles said. "We're hoping to find that out when we get the next intelligence information. That's critical information we need to analyze before we finalize our planning."

Nick punched Mack on the shoulder. "You'd better be ready for almost anything when you go over there."

"From the beginning of all this, I've been ready for almost anything," Mack said. "I'm sure everyone on the taskforce will be well prepared for a wide range of possibilities."

Charles watched everyone look at the large monitor and study the latest time-sequenced satellite reconnaissance photos from the NRO covering a wide area close to the western shore of Finland.

"Lot of possibilities, you agree?" Paul looked at

Charles and gestured toward the pictures on the monitor.

"That's why we need to send a taskforce over there," Charles said. "This isn't a situation we can handle from a distance. There are some things you must do close up and personal."

Paul gave a short laugh. "Yeah, and I think we're preparing to cover this situation from every angle." He glanced at Mack.

Mack nodded. "I'm sitting on ready."

"There are even more angles than I previously thought," Charles said. "The President told me this morning he wanted to be kept fully informed and would require briefings from us twice a day."

"Does Ken have these photos over at the FBI yet?" Nick asked, gesturing toward the monitor.

"He should have received them at the same time we did." Charles reached for the speaker phone on the table and punched a digit.

Ken answered.

After a brief opening discussion, Charles asked, "Have you had a chance to study the photos?"

"Thoroughly," Ken said, "and I've just finished discussing them with Grant. He'll be discussing them with everyone at Boswic shortly."

"Any new thoughts?" Charles asked.

"Grant told me Colt is anxious to lead the taskforce over there as soon as we can go," Ken said. "He also mentioned he had gotten the impression Linda was still anxious to go with him."

Nick and Mack each held an arm in the air, giving a thumbs-up signal.

"Looks like I have some anxious people in here with me too," Charles said. "We'll try to complete the final preparations early this afternoon and be ready to go tomorrow. You and Grant need to be ready to discuss the plan this afternoon and make any recommendations you feel are necessary. Also, have Grant tell Harlan he should be prepared to review our plan and recommend any necessary adjustments later today."

"What time this afternoon?" Ken asked.

Charles hesitated a moment and then said, "Be ready at one o'clock."

After a little more discussion Charles disconnected and looked at Paul.

"A lot of our intelligence experts think the missiles are currently on their way to those islands along Finland's coast," Charles said. "And we need to make sure everyone is well aware we'll be trying to stop the launch of two missiles, each one with a 100-megaton warhead."

"What are our experts basing their opinion on?" Paul asked.

"Multiple calls NSA has intercepted," Charles said.

"Do you know of any way we can intercept the missiles along their route to Finland?" Paul asked

Charles narrowed his eyes. "We don't know anything about the timing, the route, or the method of transportation, but the Navy has all their assets on alert around that whole area."

A brief silence ensued.

Charles knew they again had a difficult problem like the one they had resolved in Jamaica, but this time it could be even more of a challenge. He didn't want to express all his concerns at the moment and sound like an alarmist. He would continue to do his best to help things work out for the United States and hope for good results.

Chapter 9

In the Kremlin, Lev sat at the large mahogany desk in his office and looked at Yuri, who was sitting in front of him.

"We need to decide on the best way to get the two missiles to Ivan and Sergei," Lev said.

"I thought our superiors would make that decision."

Lev grunted. "I was just informed you and I need to make it."

"So, we'll be blamed if anything goes wrong?"

Lev's eyes flashed as he gave a slow nod. "That's probably the case. Our leaders want maximum deniability."

"Damn," Yuri said. "We don't have all the necessary resources at our immediate disposal like our superiors do."

"I'm told we must make the decision on the general route and mode of transportation. Our superiors will handle any necessary details that don't get properly addressed."

Yuri nodded and asked, "Do you have any good ideas

right now?"

"Yeah, I do." Lev gave a slight smile.

Yuri leaned forward.

"I'm sure China has copied the missiles and has developed their own methods to launch them," Lev said. "The new ones have super navigation controls, and they have unlimited range due to being powered by a miniature nuclear reactor. We'll ask China to program in all the navigation details and launch the missiles to the island where Ivan and Sergei have constructed their launch site for striking the United States."

Yuri brightened and gave a quick nod.

"The missiles can normally travel underwater at a speed of 80 miles an hour," Lev said. "That's faster than the nuclear-powered attack submarines of the United States and also faster than their anti-ship missiles. The Poseidon Missiles can also travel at a depth of 3,280 feet. That's far lower than any submarines can go."

Yuri continued to nod. "And China helped us improve the speed to exceed 200 miles per hour by adding ramjet engines and creating a bubble of gas for the missile to travel in."

"Finding a way to reduce friction with the water was a brilliant innovation," Lev said. "Other than flying them up there, this will be the fastest mode of transportation. And it's also the safest by far, being able to travel at 200 miles an hour at a depth of 3,280 feet will keep the missiles from being detected."

Yuri gave a dismissive wave. "I don't think anyone will argue with that logic. I think we've made our decision."

Lev pursed his lips and grunted as he picked up the phone.

Chapter 10

On his private island near the western shore of Finland, Ivan Titov sat in his office and fished an expensive Cuban cigar out of a container on his desk.

Leaning slightly forward, Ivan flicked his lighter and held the flame to the end of his cigar. He savored a long puff and then stared out the window at the heavy rain beating against the clear glass.

His phone rang at that moment.

Ivan could see it was a call from the Kremlin. He quickly reached for the phone and answered. After a brief conversation, he disconnected and again stared out the window. Despite the weather, things were looking better on many aspects of the project now.

He puffed slowly on his cigar while he waited for Sergei Nikitin to arrive for their scheduled meeting.

In a few minutes Sergei entered the room.

After Sergei hung up his wet coat, Ivan stood and

waved him toward one of the chairs at the round conference table near his desk.

"I just got some new information and I think it's good," Ivan said.

Sergei pulled the heavily padded chair away from the table and sat down. He looked expectantly at Ivan.

Ivan took a long slow puff on his cigar and then plopped down in an empty chair across from Sergei.

"Lev called and told me the two Poseidon Missiles will be launched from China to us," Ivan said. He took another puff on his cigar and looked directly at Sergei, who had narrowed his eyes.

"How can they do that?" Sergei asked.

Ivan took another puff on his cigar. "The new guidance systems are so good they can deliver them right to our door." He grinned.

There was a brief silence.

"These missiles can travel at 200 miles per hour, right?" Sergei asked.

"Right and they'll be at the bottom of the ocean for most of the trip. Remember they can reach a depth of 3,280 feet."

Sergei gave a dismissive wave. "Well, I don't think they'll be intercepted."

Ivan pursed his lips and grunted. He then leaned back and took a long puff on his cigar.

Sergei looked around the room. "I need some hot coffee."

Ivan motioned toward a side table by the window. "Help yourself." He stood and followed Sergei.

"Are Lev and Yuri making sure they'll be deactivated so they won't detonate when they get here?" Sergei asked, as he grabbed a large mug off the table and filled it with coffee.

"Yes, of course," Ivan said. "Lev assured me several experts have checked and double-checked all the necessary things." He filled a mug and walked back toward the table. "All the safety precautions have been taken. We'll make sure we don't shoot ourselves in the foot."

Sergei gave a short sarcastic laugh. "Yeah, it's good we don't do that, especially with a couple of 100 megaton bombs."

After the two men were seated again, Sergei leaned forward. "Do we know yet when to expect the delivery?"

"Within the next few days," Ivan said. "Lev told me not to sweat it. He and Yuri would keep us well informed."

"I guess we'll still need to supervise the entire process for the missile reception and setup?"

"Yes, same basic plan as before. We'll get all the necessary workers we'll need."

"Do you know who they are?"

"Lev told me we'll find out tomorrow."

"What about the computers?"

"They'll be delivered by boat within the next two days."

Sergei nodded slowly and then flashed a big smile. "I guess we'll be ready to roll before the week is over."

"Yes and Lev mentioned one other thing to keep in mind."

"What?"

"A major aspect of our project has just changed."

Sergei leaned forward.

"We're now going to hit two different target areas in the United States."

"Which ones?"

"Tampa will still be a target, of course," Ivan said, "and now we'll also hit Washington DC."

Sergei exhaled sharply and spilled a little coffee on the table.

"Everything will work smoothly, you'll see," Ivan said. "Everything is being carefully planned."

"It was carefully planned last time."

"Lev assured me everyone in the Kremlin will be even more careful on this project. They'll take every measure to make sure all our plans are foolproof."

Sergei nodded slowly and didn't comment.

"As before, our project will need a lot of funding and we'll get it through dummy corporations which will appear as legitimate organizations involved in international projects run by various global entities," Ivan said.

Sergei narrowed his eyes. "The Americans might be catching on to what we're doing."

"Why do you say that?"

Sergei gave a slight shrug. "I guess because we've been doing it a long time. I don't think we can keep pulling it off forever. This is a huge undertaking, and our tactics might need to cover a really broad area at times. We'll constantly be spending a lot of money. That could attract attention."

"Maybe, but we have other people who will worry about that, very smart people," Ivan said. "Don't forget, we're not responsible for developing the strategy. We just have to follow orders. We just have to develop the specific tactics we'll use for launching the missiles and then execute."

"Speaking of tactics, being responsible for making sure the underwater missiles are launched successfully isn't a small task," Sergei replied. "We have a lot of responsibility for a huge variety of technical, financial, and security aspects." He stared at Ivan.

Ivan made a dismissive wave. "I'm sure we can handle it. Are you still game?"

"Of course," Sergei said, "but only if we're a lot more careful this time."

"I'm sure we will be," Ivan replied. "This time we'll make sure we get the missiles launched and blow the hell out of the Americans."

Chapter 11

Early the next morning, Colt and Linda sat with Harlan and Jim at the round conference table in Harlan's office.

"We have a lot to discuss and some decisions to make about our priorities," Harlan said. He scanned the faces around the table. "I've received some new information from Grant that confirms some things we've suspected."

Colt noted the determined look on both Harlan's and Jim's faces. He figured the expressions had something to do with what they were going to discuss.

Harlan looked at Colt. "Charles Andrews wants you to again command the taskforce he's putting together. You'll lead the team in the field and again have to keep some Poseidon Missiles from being launched and striking the United States."

Colt nodded.

"Like when you were in Jamaica, it's probable you'll again have to deal with a large number of skilled assassins," Jim said, "along with an assortment of hi-tech gadgets and computers."

Colt continued to nod.

Jim looked at Linda.

She also nodded.

Harlan narrowed his eyes and studied Colt for a moment. "Charles still has a high opinion of you. You game?"

"Yes, of course" Colt said.

Harlan and Jim each gave a thumbs-up and turned toward Linda.

"Are you asking me the same question?" Linda asked.

"Yes," Harlan said. "And as usual, you'll need to stay with Colt step by step and back him up."

Linda gave a slight smile. "I can do that and yes I'm game."

"Blake will continue to work closely with both of you and provide a lot of research and analysis," Jim said. "As usual, he'll also work closely with all the intelligence agencies."

Harlan leaned forward. "Do either of you have any questions?"

Linda narrowed her eyes. "From various things you told us earlier, it sounds like our Military is going to be more involved this time. Is that correct?"

"The Navy will be more involved in surveillance of the waterways," Harlan said, "but, like before, our Armed Forces will only get directly involved if we fail. The President still wants to try an all-civilian approach first and avoid another world war if possible."

"So, he thinks our taskforce will be capable of resolving this?" Colt asked.

Jim shrugged. "He knows we were successful last time, and he obviously wants to try it again."

"Resolving the wide a range of issues is still going to be quite a challenge," Linda said. "But we did it before."

Harlan leaned forward. "You and Colt have already

proven capable of resolving this level of threats and we didn't start another world war. It's clear the President is comfortable in giving you another shot at it."

Colt and Linda each gave a thumbs-up.

"Getting involved in projects like this is what we're in business for." Harlan wrinkled his brow. "However, this one is starting out a little more dangerous than usual. NSA has picked up bits and pieces of multiple phone conversations coming from those islands just off the western shore of Finland into various locations in the United States. Assassins were mentioned, assassins to knock off the Americans."

"And those Americans include us, right?" Colt asked while making a sweeping gesture which included both him and Linda.

Harlan nodded. "And they're still after you in particular."

There was a brief silence.

Harlan's gaze took in both Colt and Linda. "We need to review the latest threat matrix Grant sent over." He mashed a button on a control in front of him and gestured toward a large monitor on the wall. "We need to keep a lot of things in mind when the taskforce goes over to Finland's western shore, and we need to remember Ivan Titov owns some of those islands"

Jim pointed at a group of segmented images on the monitor. "You can see he has at least two islands set up with security cameras, motion detectors, no-trespassing signs, boat piers, helipads, and swimming pools, all draped with camouflage netting. He has enough housing for a small army."

"Do we know yet if he actually has a small army there?" Linda asked.

"Probably," Jim said. "Based on NRO feedback we've been getting; we know black speedboats packed with men dressed in camouflage fatigues have been seen constantly docking at all of the piers on a couple of islands. It looks like there's constant military-like activity."

"We fought the equivalent of a small army in Jamaica," Colt said. "This won't be any different."

Harlan and Jim both stared at Colt. "It probably will have some new challenges you'll need to be prepared for."

"Such as?" Colt asked. He figured the threat matrix presented everyday to Grant Winston, the local FBI chief, was becoming more ominous by the hour. He knew Grant maintained close coordination with the CIA concerning all the events Boswic was expected to be involved with.

Harlan rubbed his chin slowly and looked at Jim. "Go ahead and lead this discussion. You and I both just discussed all the details with Grant."

Jim turned fully toward the large screen on the wall that now displayed another group of satellite images. He used a laser pointer to highlight an area on one of the islands and then glanced at Colt and Linda.

"It looks like they're building the missile launching structure here," Jim said. "We'll see how things develop, but that's probably the first location you'll go to."

Both Colt and Linda nodded.

"An army will probably be waiting for you to show up, but we don't know what their strategy will be," Jim said. "We'll try to get more insight into that as soon as we can. NSA will keep trying to intercept as many calls as they can and decrypt them as soon as possible."

Harlan scanned the faces around the table. "Grant mentioned he was anxiously awaiting the next update. He hopes we'll soon get a lot more details on every aspect of what we're dealing with."

"A ton of Russian experts in the Kremlin know a lot about us and they've proven to be smart people," Jim said. "I think we should expect a lot more surprises this time."

There was a brief silence.

Harlan narrowed his eyes and focused on Colt and

Linda.

"We can expect they'll be smarter in every way this time," Harlan said. "Many of them probably have a personal grudge now. The more you know about every damned aspect of this, the safer you'll be." He paused for several moments. "Grant told us the Russians have already implemented their new initiative which they've named Project Neptune."

Jim leaned forward and said, "We need to outsmart them on every aspect of what they plan to do."

Chapter 12

On his private island in the archipelago off the western shore of Finland, Ivan sat in the desk chair in his office and thought about the upcoming project the Kremlin had named Project Neptune.

He had a second chance to succeed in bringing down the United States. There was a lot to think about.

Ivan knew the chess masters in Moscow who were developing the strategy would consider all possible countermoves the Americans would make. Then the game would become more like poker. He and Sergei would make the necessary tactical adjustments as things progressed.

After leaning back in his chair, Ivan chuckled.

He was confident the Americans would never figure out all the details of the plan his team would be using. His team would have too many options and they would use the computers to thoroughly analyze all the options constantly. He and Sergei would always make any necessary changes to their plan and keep it at an optimum level.

Their strategy was good and this time he planned on executing it successfully.

Money was again a big factor in what they were doing and this time they would succeed in hacking into the Federal Reserve System.

Ivan continued to chuckle. The Americans were now going to get a run on their financial system they would never detect, until it was too late.

He reflected on the situation.

The American Federal Reserve System was created in 1913 as a response to prior financial panics and bank runs.

He remembered the Federal Reserve advertised four duties: The first was to conduct the nation's monetary policy by influencing monetary and credit conditions in the economy. Next the Fed supervised and regulated banking institutions to ensure the soundness of the nation's systems. Then they maintained stability by containing systemic risk.

Lastly, they provided financial services to depository institutions and played a major role in operating the nation's payments system.

Ivan continued to chuckle as he considered the overall situation.

This last role of the Federal Reserve System was the one he planned to take full advantage of. The new transactions the Fed would be handling would look like normal business. The dummy corporations Moscow and Beijing had established would again provide the funding his team needed.

His team would receive billions of dollars to finish the construction needed for better defense and missile launching on his island and maybe some other islands around him.

Soon he would have it all set up.

Ivan went from a chuckle to a huge laugh. He liked the way things were progressing.

"What's so amusing?" Sergei asked as he walked

through the doorway into Ivan's office and eased into the chair in front of Ivan's desk.

"Your timing is perfect. I was sitting here reviewing our strategy and tactics for our new activity. Things are looking good."

"Do we have another financial expert and another computer expert yet?" Sergei asked.

"Two men will be joining us later today," Ivan said. "Lev told me they've both been approved by the Kremlin." He looked directly at Sergei. "And each one is both a financial experts and a computer expert."

"What are their names?"

"Dmitri Fedorov and Pavel Werner," Ivan said. "Each one of them can handle any needed tasks with the computers and the funding."

"Do you have all the details yet about where the money we'll receive is coming from?"

"I asked but I didn't get any new details," Ivan said. "You and I both know the general strategy. Remember we don't need to worry about our master plan. We just need to follow orders, and we're being paid very well to do that. We just need to make the necessary tactical decisions as things progress."

Sergei nodded. "Yeah, but that would be easier if we knew more of the overall details."

"Why does that matter as long as we get the money?"

Sergei shrugged.

"Are you still worried about not getting paid at some point in time?" Ivan asked.

"Do we still have the responsibility of paying any of the people who'll be working for us?"

Ivan leaned forward. "Why are you still worried about the funding? We never had a problem getting our money and making our payroll down in Jamaica."

Sergei gave a slight shrug. "I'm just thinking about everything. We might need to take more precautions as we go forward. We definitely need to pay attention to details."

"Don't worry. I'm sure everyone will get paid, especially us."

Sergei looked at Ivan with an expression of concern on his face. "We know Randall is capable of screwing everything up."

"He probably won't be involved in any of the money situation, and he might not come over here, besides he's going to be eliminated real soon anyway."

"Maybe," Sergei said.

"Why are you so skeptical all of a sudden?" Ivan asked.

"I've been reviewing a lot of things we'll need to do, and I think we're going to have to be real careful we don't leave a lot of loose ends that could cause us some big problems later on. Randall is definitely a loose end."

Ivan leaned forward. "I told you he's going to be eliminated."

"I'll believe it when it's done."

"We'll make sure we check everything multiple times as we move forward from step to step."

Sergei gave a dismissive wave. "Maybe things will work out."

Ivan pursed his lips and grunted.

There was a brief silence.

"Any update about when we can expect to receive the missiles?" Sergei asked.

"No update, but we know it should be within the week."

"So, what's our current number one priority?"

"We'll sit down with Dmitri and Pavel this afternoon and make sure we're in sync on what to do relative to our finances and the computers."

"Are they going to check all the details on the funding?"

"Yes and they'll coordinate directly with Lev and Yuri

on that. We don't need to get into the details. We just have to make sure the computers are setup and ready to function."

Sergei narrowed his eyes and made no comment.

"Everything will work smoothly," Ivan said. "We're well set up. You'll see." He gave a sly grin.

Sergei nodded slowly and remained silent.

Chapter 13

Lev sat at the desk in his office in the Kremlin and thought about what was immediately ahead on the project his superiors in the Kremlin had appropriately named Project Neptune.

A lot of things needed to be done, and done with precision.

Yuri would be joining him soon. There was a lot they needed to discuss after the failure in Jamaica. His superiors in the Kremlin thought there was now a need for closer supervision of the activities to launch the missiles.

He knew the quantum computer and the supercomputer might be installed in Ivan's headquarters on his private Island. They would be more protected there. However, he remembered Ivan had mentioned he might install them in the two missilc structures and that they would be just as secure there and maybe even more secure since they would be separated from the constant communication flowing from the headquarters.

Lev gave a mental shrug. He and Yuri had both recommended to their superiors in the Kremlin that the computers be installed in a secure location in Moscow, but their superiors hadn't agreed. He would let Ivan do what he thought was best. He and Yuri would wait and see what happened.

Their new computer and financial specialists, Dmitri and Pavel would be joining Ivan and Sergei on the island this afternoon. Both specialists would be directly involved in all the computer hacking and financial maneuvering. He and Yuri had instructions to monitor everything the specialists were doing. Obviously his superiors thought it was necessary for him and Yuri to stay on top of everything going on with the computers and the finances. If they all executed correctly, the CIA would never know what the Russians had done. Neither would the FBI or anyone else, especially the Federal Reserve and the United States Mint.

After taking a deep breath, Lev exhaled slowly and continued his thought process.

Their new project, Project Neptune, needed a lot of new funding. Maybe the Chinese would have to be closely involved in that again? He would ask his superiors the next time they talked.

It would be best if the Federal Reserve never knew a lot of their money was stolen. If the heist was executed properly, the Fed's records would show the money went to seemingly legitimate corporations (who were really dummy corporations) who would be camouflaged by fake activities with the World Bank. The dummy corporations would appear as legitimate organizations involved in international projects run by various countries.

Lev thought again about the chess masters in Moscow who were developing the strategy. They would certainly consider all possible countermoves the Americans would make and prepare accordingly. Things would have to be foolproof to have absolute certainty of success.

While considering things for another moment, Lev laughed. He was confident the Americans would never figure out all the details of the plan his team would be using. His team would have too many options and they would use the new computers to thoroughly analyze all the options at each step in the process. They would, of course, always select the optimal one.

Lev continued to laugh. The American Federal Reserve System would get a financial drain they would never detect, until it was too late.

The new transactions the Fed would be handling would look like normal business. The dummy corporations would provide the funding his team needed under the guise of doing necessary work for various world organizations.

His team would receive billions of dollars to construct all the necessary facilities to secretly launch the new upgraded Poseidon Missiles.

"Are you ready to jump into all the details of how we're going to make our project succeed?" Yuri asked as he rushed through the open doorway into Lev's office.

"Of course, I was just sitting here reviewing our strategy and tactics while I was waiting for you."

"Have you talked to Dmitri and Pavel?"

Lev glanced at his watch. "I'll call them before they have their meeting with Ivan and Sergei."

There was a brief silence.

"Do we have a firm schedule yet?" Yuri asked.

"There are still a lot of variables being worked out," Lev said. "I'm told by our superiors we'll get a schedule soon."

"How soon?"

"I'm told before the end of the day tomorrow."

"Any new issues I should know about?"

"I received the usual intelligence briefing. It was all about planning ahead to take over the United States, all the regular stuff. I didn't get any new details."

"Do you have any more information about where the money is coming from to fund all of our activity?"

"Why does that matter as long as we get the money?"

Yuri shrugged. "It would be good to know what the process will be."

"Do you have any worries about everybody getting paid?" Lev asked.

"Maybe," Yuri said. He leaned forward. "Who has the responsibility of paying all of the people who'll be working for us on this new project, including all of the security, assassins included?"

"Ivan and Sergei will have the responsibility for making the actual payments. We have the responsibility to make sure they have the money."

"People, especially the assassins, who don't get their money can get pretty vicious. Those of us in charge all need to understand the details for the process we'll use."

"I don't think you should waste your time worrying about any of that. I'm confident everyone will get paid, especially us."

Yuri leaned forward. "Randall is still around and we know he can screw everything up."

"He probably won't be involved in any of the money situation, besides he's going to be eliminated real soon anyway. Our assassins this time will be even better than the ones who were working on The Poseidon Initiative."

"Maybe."

"Why are you so skeptical?" Lev asked.

"I've been reviewing everything we have going on too." Yuri narrowed his eyes. "Ivan and Sergei didn't do such a good job before."

"Do you think we should get rid of them?"

"We'll keep that in mind as we see how things develop."

Lev narrowed his eyes as he stared at Yuri. "Don't

forget, they're not responsible for developing the strategy. They just have to follow orders. They just have to make on-the-spot decisions about the specific tactics to use and then execute."

"I'm not sure they made very good on-the-spot decisions last time. If we decide they didn't, we can't tolerate that again."

"They'll probably be a lot smarter this time. I'm sure they learned a lot from their experiences down in Jamaica."

There was a brief silence.

"This is another huge undertaking, and our tactics might need to cover an even broader area than before," Yuri said. "We all have a lot of responsibility for a huge variety of strategic, technical, financial, and security aspects. We must make sure the missiles not only get launched, but that they hit their precise targets."

Lev shrugged. "We all know that. I think we should give Ivan and Sergei another chance."

Yuri pursed his lips and then asked, "Are you sure we'll have plenty of funding to install every new innovation we'll need on each of our islands in that archipelago?"

"We'll review that as soon as we talk to Dmitri and Pavel."

"You and I need to make sure we know everything we need and get the approval of our superiors here in the Kremlin before we talk to them about the funding."

Lev leaned back in his chair and stared at the ceiling for a few moments. He took a deep breath and exhaled slowly.

"You know I'm right," Yuri said emphatically.

A brief silence ensued.

"We have a pretty complete list right now and everything has been approved by our superiors here in the Kremlin," Lev said. "I suggest we discuss all that with Dmitri and Pavel in our phone conversation and then they can discuss everything again during their meeting with Ivan and Sergei." He stared at Yuri for several moments.

There was another brief silence.

Yuri seemed to be thinking. After a couple of minutes, he nodded slowly.

"If anything new comes up we want to add to the list, we'll call our superiors and ask for approval. We all must stay closely coordinated."

After a long hesitation, Yuri gave a slight smile. "I think that should work okay."

Chapter 14

At Boswic in Tampa, Colt, Linda, and Blake sat with Harlan and Jim at the large table in the main conference room.

"Mack just flew down from Washington," Harlan said. "He and Grant will join us within the next few minutes."

"Anything special we're going to talk about?" Colt asked.

"We'll discuss and refine our plan to send the taskforce up to that area along the west coast of Finland," Harlan said. "Grant assured me Mack would have all the latest intelligence the CIA has gathered. And Grant also mentioned Ken had sent him all the latest intelligence the FBI has gathered."

Jim scanned the faces around the table. "So, we should be in good shape to start putting together all the details of how we're going to contend with this latest initiative by the Russians."

"Are the Chinese still involved?" Linda asked.

"I don't know," Harlan said, "hopefully Mack will have the latest information about that."

There was a brief silence.

"I'm guessing the Chinese are still very much involved," Jim said. "They want to bring us down more than Russia does. I don't think it will matter whether Russia wants them participating in this new project or not. I think the Chinese will find a way to get into the middle of the activity."

Harlan nodded. "I can't argue with that."

Everyone else also nodded.

"One thing for sure," Harlan said. "We need to make sure neither the Russians nor the Chinese succeed in blowing the hell out of us."

Everyone looked toward the doorway as Mack and Grant were escorted into the conference room.

Mack said, "I have all the latest intelligence the CIA could compile. There's one hell of a lot going on."

Colt watched the two men plop into two empty chairs at the table while Mack continued talking.

"We've verified Ivan Titov will use his private island as the launch site for the Poseidon Missiles. NSA and NRO both have a lot of new evidence."

"Can you elaborate?" Colt asked.

"NRO has satellite images of several new facilities being built on the water's edge," Mack said. "NSA has also intercepted some phone calls from Moscow to that island where various people discuss the plans."

"Why would they take the chance of their calls being intercepted?" Harlan asked.

"The Russians apparently think their calls are totally secure now," Mack said. "NSA told me decrypting the calls has become more difficult, but they're still able to do it."

Blake leaned forward. "I bet the Russians are using some new software from China and the Chinese experts in Beijing assured them that it was totally secure."

Linda gave a short laugh and then said, "Sounds about right."

"Did the Russians say much about launching the missiles?" Jim asked.

"Quite a bit," Mack said. "It looks like they're definitely launching two missiles that are 100 megatons each. They can do unthinkable damage, and we have to stop them."

"Do we know the targets yet?" Harlan asked.

"Tampa and Washington DC," Mack said.

"Washington DC is logical but why Tampa?" Colt asked.

Grant looked directly at Colt and said, "Two reasons, you and MacDill Air Force Base."

Colt gave a slow nod. "I guess their desire for revenge is stronger than I thought." He narrowed his eyes. "I never thought they would waste a 100-megaton bomb just to get me."

"I'm sure they don't think they're wasting it," Grant said. "There are a lot of strategic assets in the general area and MacDill isn't small potatoes." He continued to stare at Colt. "You've been a thorn in their side for a long time. I guess you tipped the scale in favor of the Tampa area being one of the two targets."

Blake nodded. "I think this whole strategy has once more been cooked up by the chess masters in Moscow. And I'm sure they've been working with the hoard of strategist in the Kremlin to finalize the current plan."

"So, you think the chess masters are still deeply involved in the strategy developed by the Kremlin?" Linda asked.

Blake nodded. "I have no doubt."

"NSA has collected a lot of information that verifies that's the case," Mack said. "The chess masters were heavily involved in the strategy and the tactics at the beginning of all this and they still are."

Colt's glance took in both Mack and Grant. "Do you think hitting Tampa was part of a backup plan the chess masters developed earlier?"

Mack leaned forward. "Yeah I do, and now I think they've moved it to the forefront because you led the taskforce that defeated them in Jamaica." He looked directly at Colt. "You also led the taskforce that defeated them when they partnered with the Mexican drug cartels. I think they've decided you must be eliminated no matter what the costs."

Grant gave a short laugh. "That's definitely the way the analysts at the FBI have it figured."

There was a brief silence.

"I think we're simply looking at another iteration of Russia's and China's joint initiative to bring the United States down," Harlan said, "getting rid of obstacles in their path has now become a major undertaking."

Jim looked at Mack and Grant. "And this new initiative we're facing is called Project Neptune?"

"That's correct," Mack said. "And since we'll get more military support this time, everything is in progress to finalize the coordination with the appropriate governments, especially those of Sweden and Finland. We'll defeat the villains again regardless of how well they prepare."

Harlan grunted. "China is probably still involved in all aspects of this, the technology, the weapons, the money, the planning, and the execution." He leaned toward Mack. "Like I've mentioned a few times before, we need to keep following the money no matter how well they cover their tracks."

Everyone nodded.

Colt knew things were going to quickly escalate, that was a no-brainer. He knew they would need to move fast to prevent a huge catastrophe.

Chapter 15

In the Kremlin, Lev sat with Yuri at a round conference table in his office. He removed a phone from his pocket and then punched in a number. He heard Dmitri answer.

"Are you and Pavel still meeting with Ivan and Sergei?" Lev asked.

"In about two hours," Dmitri said.

"Yuri and I want to talk to both of you first for about thirty minutes. Can you spare the time?"

"Yes."

"Is Pavel there with you?"

"Yes."

"Put your phone on speaker and we'll get started."

In a few seconds, Lev asked, "Have you put the funding in place to start building the necessary missile launching structures on the island where Ivan has his headquarters?"

"Yes, and they've already started on the construction," Dmitri said. "Pavel and I will discuss all that in our meeting with them. We'll plan to cover all the details and reach agreement on the exact schedule from this point on. We're using mobile missile launching structures utilizing the latest technology and we can make a wide range of adjustments if we should need to."

"That's good. The more flexibility we have the better," Lev said.

There was a brief silence.

"We have another issue to deal with. Something else just came up," Lev said.

"Does this have anything to do with Colt Randall?" Dmitri paused for a moment. "He's been a huge problem for us in the past."

"You work for us as a financial and computer specialist. Why are you concerned about Randall?" Lev asked.

"He screwed everything up the Kremlin was trying to do before and all the computer work involved was impacted," Dmitri said. "Pavel and I both think he needs to be eliminated as soon as possible."

"None of our intelligence agents think Randall is involved with any computer activity at this time," Yuri said. "But we all know he'll impact everything we have going on if their taskforce comes to Finland."

"And that's why I'm concerned," Pavel said. "Our assassins need to make sure he never gets to any of our strategic sites up here. We can't allow him to lead another effort to shut us down."

"Yeah and right now our moles think Randall is going to lead another taskforce being setup to combat the latest threats," Lev replied. "They speculate the taskforce will be coming to the area in and around the archipelago to prevent the launch of the missiles."

"Will the moles keep us informed about the progress of the taskforce?" Dmitri asked.

"As much as they can," Yuri said.

"If they do come to Ivan's base, we can't let them shut our facilities down like they've done before." Dmitri narrowed his eyes. "We can't let Randall live long enough to lead them again."

"Yuri and I will work closely with Ivan and Sergei to get rid of Randall as soon as possible," Lev said. "We have another group of expert assassins to send to protect you, and we have a lot of options on how to deploy them."

There was a brief silence.

"Do you know yet when the missiles will be delivered?" Pavel asked with a hint of concern in his voice.

"It should be within the next three days," Yuri said. "You and Dmitri should discuss this with Ivan and Sergei. You should make sure you're ready to get them in the launchers immediately and start the reprogramming of all the necessary controls. We don't want any unnecessary delays."

"And speaking of the reprogramming, how long do you think it will take?" Lev asked.

"Probably around four days," Dmitri said. "There's a lot to do. We have to program two different routes and two different detonation points. Everything must be extremely precise. We don't want any premature explosions."

Lev watched Yuri winch.

"Do you need more help on that?" Yuri asked.

"We have all the experts we can use," Dmitri said. "Pavel and I will be supervising the process. He'll concentrate on the routing, and I'll concentrate on ensuring the explosions occur at the optimal locations. Like we said, everything must be extremely precise. We can't rush things and make a mistake."

Lev grunted. "Yeah, we can't make any mistakes."

"We still have to move with the utmost speed," Yuri said. "We need to finish everything and launch before the American taskforce gets there."

"Can't you do some things to slow them down?" Pavel asked.

"We're working on a lot of possibilities," Lev said.

"We'll pick some of our best options soon. We'll work closely with Ivan and Sergei on that and keep everyone informed."

"Do you know yet if any Chinese are going to be working with us in the area around Finland?" Dmitri asked.

"Our superiors in the Kremlin told us they had a lot of conversations with Beijing about that," Lev said. "I asked a lot of questions, and I didn't get any definite answers. However, they assured us they were working closely with all the top Chinese officials, and we would be getting specific information as things developed. Of course we'll keep you informed."

"Any guesses?" Pavel asked.

"I think the Chinese Government wants to have firsthand knowledge of exactly what we do step by step so they can offer support in needed areas to ensure we succeed," Lev said. "It's logical they would have some of their key people involved directly with us. Remember, our success against the United States is also their success."

Lev watched Yuri nod slowly.

Another brief silence ensued.

"I think we've discussed things enough for now," Yuri said. "Go have your meeting with Ivan and Sergei and then we'll all discuss things again. All of us will certainly need to stay in close touch as things progress."

Chapter 16

At Boswic in Tampa, Colt and Linda sat with Blake at the small round conference table in Colt's office.

Colt wanted to discuss more details about the technical aspects of the upcoming mission before their scheduled meeting in the main conference room with Harlan and Jim.

"Would you bring us up to date on a lot of these matters we're going to be dealing with?" Colt asked.

"And include your latest discussions with all the other experts on the subjects," Linda said as she smiled and leaned slightly toward Blake.

Blake nodded and gave a quick summary.

"So, you still think the game of chess serves as the metaphor for the ongoing strategy we're facing?" Colt asked.

"Everyone agrees we're dealing with the thinking of three chess masters working in the Kremlin," Blake said. "And everyone agrees China is still directly involved. And it looks like China is still allowing Russia to do all the strategic planning."

Colt looked directly at Blake. "We've talked about this before and both Linda and I think chess analogies might be useful in developing strategies, but we think they're not so useful in executing them."

Blake gave a slow nod and didn't comment.

"We think poker expertise can be a big help when you're in the field and having to make quick decisions," Linda said. "In chess, the pieces are in plain sight on the board at all times. When you're playing poker, you don't know what the opposing hands are. You must deal with a lot of incomplete information like we always have to contend with in the heat of battle."

"I've never argued with you about that." Blake's glance took in both Colt and Linda. "But the Russians obviously think using chess strategy helps them get off to a good start on formulating the overall plan they're going to use. And I still like using chess strategy because it helps me anticipate the strategy the Russians have set up. If we can anticipate their strategy, we can adjust our tactics accordingly."

"Logical enough," Colt said. He hesitated a moment and then asked, "Have you formed an opinion yet of what our primary task should be when we get up to Titov's headquarters area?"

"I think it will be the same as it was in Jamaica. You'll need to find the exact launch site or sites for the Poseidon Missiles. I haven't yet been able to determine conclusively from the surveillance photos where any launch sites are. I've found no obvious launch equipment yet." Blake tightened his lips. "The CIA and FBI analysts have the same problem. If things don't change, our taskforce will have to do that job after you get up there. It looks like you'll have a similar situation to what you had before."

Colt nodded and waited for Blake to continue.

"It looks like the Kremlin still wants to take aggressive action and stay in a position to deny any responsibility for any aggressive activity toward the United States," Blake said.

"What about China?" Linda asked.

"That seems to be the case with them too," Blake said. "They can admit to improving the Poseidon Missiles and still deny any involvement in launching them." He shrugged.

There was a brief silence.

Colt glanced at his watch. "It's about time for our scheduled meeting with Harlan and Jim. I guess we should prepare to be on our way."

"They've probably received some more information. Hopefully we can firm up all the latest details for the taskforce mission," Blake said.

Colt nodded as he stood and moved toward the doorway.

Linda and Blake followed.

Chapter 17

On his private island in the archipelago just off the western shore of Finland, Ivan sat at the large table in his main conference room with a large window and a view of the water as he prepared to start his meeting with the five other people sitting around him.

Sergei, Dmitri, and Pavel were there and so were three master assassins, Roman Arnold, Yan Block, and Eduard Sidorov.

“Colt Randall and the American taskforce will be coming in the next few days,” Ivan said. “I just received confirmation of that from one of our moles in Washington DC.”

Sergei nodded. “And, as before, Randall will lead their taskforce.”

“Will the moles be able to keep us informed on the progress of this new taskforce?” Dmitri asked.

“That’s the plan,” Ivan said. “All of them are doing a

lot of internal maneuvering to constantly stay in a position to do that."

Pavel gestured toward the three assassins. "Are they going to confront Randall?"

"Of course," Ivan said, "But maybe not before he gets here. We'll see how thing work out."

"I'd like to go over to the United States and eliminate him before he leaves to come here," Roman said. He stared at Ivan. "I'm talented enough to do that."

Ivan shrugged. "We've never been successful trying to do that before."

"What do we have to lose?" Roman asked.

"That could result in our having one less world-class assassin to help defend things up here." Ivan returned Roman's stare.

Roman narrowed his eyes. "I can pull it off. I guarantee it. I've been looking forward to kicking his ass and it will be a lot better to do it before he gets over here."

Sergei leaned toward Roman. "Do you have a plan?"

"Not yet, I'll work one out while I'm on my way over there," Roman said emphatically. "I've been thinking about a few things in that regard."

"Such as?" Sergei asked.

"You want to eliminate him as quickly as possible, of course," Roman said. "If the moles will help me pin down his exact location, I'll plan to be quick, and he'll no longer be a problem for us to worry about." Roman turned both palms up and gave a slight shrug as he scanned the faces around the table.

"Do you have anything specific in mind?" Sergei asked.

"Like I told you, I'll work that out," Roman said. "I want to have the first chance to eliminate Randall. I know all about him and I hate that bastard."

"I'm sure you'll get your chance, but you might have to wait until he gets over here," Ivan said.

Roman gazed out at the water and clinched a fist. "I'm a better fighter than Randall and I'm ready to prove it."

Ivan looked directly at Roman. "We'll keep in mind what you want to do. We'll see how things work out. Right now, we have some more things to discuss."

Roman gave a slight nod and made no comment.

Ivan's gaze took in both Dmitri and Pavel. "Our computers are set up. Are you okay with trying to hack into the Federal Reserve System as soon as you can?"

"We have all the details worked out," Dmitri said. "Pavel and I can handle it, and we'll make sure we succeed this time."

"We can still get a lot of help from Chinese experts if we want it," Ivan said as he leaned toward his two technical specialists.

"Have you already had discussions about that?" Pavel asked.

"Two of their top experts on the quantum computer and the Poseidon Missiles are ready to travel here if we want them," Ivan said. "They know all the latest stuff about using the quantum computer to manage the missile guidance systems."

Pavel glanced at Dmitri.

Dmitri gave a slight shrug with one shoulder.

Pavel looked back at Ivan. "Dmitri and I might know them. What are their names?"

"Chung Ming and Fu Wong," Ivan said as he looked curiously toward Pavel and Dmitri.

"We've both worked with Fu Wong," Pavel said. "I don't know the other man." He again glanced at Dmitri.

"I remember reading some of his research," Dmitri replied. "I have the impression he's a real expert on the use of quantum computers for missile guidance systems."

"Should we bring them on board then?" Sergei asked.

"They could probably be of some help, and this is a critical time to make sure we have everything right." Dmitri looked directly at Pavel.

Pavel leaned toward Ivan. “How soon can they be here?”

“I’m told they’re packed and prepared to leave immediately upon our request for them to join us,” Ivan said.

Dmitri and Pavel again looked at each other and then looked at Ivan as they each gave a thumb-up.”

Ivan picked up his phone and made a call. After he disconnected, he looked at Dmitri and Pavel. “They’ll be on their way within the hour. They should arrive here early tomorrow morning.”

“Even with a lot of expert help, trying to do too much in a short period of time worries me,” Pavel said. “We can’t afford to rush things and make some huge mistakes.”

Sergei nodded. “Yeah, there are too many critical things going on for us to rush any of them. We can’t let anything get screwed up. We must be precise on our execution.” He stared at Ivan.

Ivan narrowed his eyes. “I’ll make sure we’re as careful as we need to be, but we need to remember we weren’t fast enough in Jamaica. We don’t want the same thing to happen again.”

Everyone gave a slow nod, but no one made any comments.

“We have a lot to do in a short period of time,” Ivan said. “We have to make sure we stay tightly coordinated.” He looked at Dmitri and Pavel. “Again, make sure you let me know immediately when the missiles are here.”

Pavel leaned forward, elbows on table. “We’ll certainly do that. After the missiles get here, do you want to be kept informed of every little detail as our work progresses?”

“Are you and Dmitri going to be watching everything that’s going on?” Ivan asked.

“We’ll have a new team of scientists working full time

on getting the missiles ready to launch. The scientists are already here and prepared to immediately start work on the missiles as soon as they're pulled out of the water and put in place," Pavel said. "Dmitri and I have worked with all of them before and we trust them completely to take care of all the details for storing and preparing the two missiles at the launch site."

Ivan furrowed his brow. "Does that mean you're not going to keep a close eye on every aspect of what they'll be doing?"

Dmitri gave a short laugh. "No, that just means Pavel and I can be selective in what we choose to check closely."

Pavel nodded. "If we find any problems, we'll immediately start checking everything the team of scientists is doing."

Dmitri's gaze took in both Ivan and Sergei. "Like we mentioned, we have complete confidence in what our team of scientists will be doing, but we'll still spot check critical items as the work progresses."

Pavel continued to nod. "Dmitri and I will stay on top of things, and we'll make sure the work progresses at a fast pace. We'll make sure the missiles will not only be reliable for hitting their intended targets, but they'll also be ready to launch as early as possible."

"All of us have to keep track of every significant detail about what's going on as things progress," Ivan said. "Then we need to compare notes often. That's the only way Sergei and I can all make the correct tactical decisions as things evolve."

Pavel and Dmitri each gave a slow nod.

"Are you expecting everything to get real complicated for us here in this area?" Dmitri asked.

"That's a definite possibility," Ivan said. "We know a taskforce is coming and Colt Randall will be leading it. He was a major factor in shutting down the last two big Russian projects." He looked at the three assassins. "We'll spend time during the rest of this meeting discussing how we want to address that."

All three assassins nodded.

Roman gestured toward Yan and Eduard. "None of us were involved in the action down in Jamaica. But the assassins who were there took Randall too lightly and didn't prepare as well as they should have. We won't make that same mistake."

"That's good and we'll count on that." Ivan looked at Sergei. "You're coordinating all of our defense preparations, right?"

Sergei gave a thumbs-up and glanced at the three assassins. "I'll make sure you're ready to get started as soon as we finish this meeting." He looked at Roman. "We'll decide whether you go after Randall in the United States or wait until he comes here."

Roman narrowed his eyes but made no comment.

Chapter 18

At Boswic in Tampa, Colt, Linda, and Blake walked into the main conference room for the scheduled meeting. Colt noted there were more attendees than he had expected.

Grant sat at the large table with Harlan and Jim. Paul Collins, head of the Terrorist Threat Investigation Unit at the CIA, also sat at the table.

"We're fortunate Paul could fly down and join us, much better than a phone conversation," Harlan said. "He has a lot of new information relative to the big picture. We'll cover some of that before we discuss the details for our upcoming mission to Finland." Harlan gestured to Paul.

Paul scanned the faces around the table. "One of our intelligence agencies found some polymorphic spyware in the Federal Reserve System that could only have been produced by a quantum computer."

"How do we know that?" Blake asked.

"It's a long story and I don't have Nick here right now

to explain the technical details," Paul said. "I don't think we should spend time on that anyway. The important thing is that it looks like the Russians, and probably the Chinese too, are at it again."

"Does this relate to what we'll be doing in Finland?" Colt asked.

Paul gestured toward the wall-mounted monitor. "Watch the screen." He pushed a key on the laptop in front of him and the screen on the wall displayed a strange image.

"This screen shows an image of an unusual computer bug," Paul said. "It's a virus that can morph into millions of digital signatures to avoid detection. We were lucky to be able to detect it."

"Any damage to the Federal Reserve System?" Jim asked.

"None detectable yet," Paul said. "We've lost no money and I suspect this one was just a test. We think we've deleted all of it, but we can't be sure. We could have missed some of the morphed parts." He looked at Colt. "If you find any computers up there in the area around Finland, let us know and we'll send the necessary specialists to inspect everything as soon as the area is safe."

Colt nodded.

Paul looked at Blake. "While we're on the subject, have you studied those new regression theorems Nick sent you?"

"A little," Blake said. "It's easy to get lost. Nick's more of an expert on the mathematics of all this than I am."

"I know he's continued his research involving Brownian motion of the oscillator involving random forces and Gaussian operators in various equations." Paul looked up from some notes on a sheet of paper in front of him and flashed a big grin. "I didn't understand much of anything from what he told me, but he mentioned he would continue to review his findings on all the relevant aspects of this with you."

"I'll try to keep up on how all the computer stuff might affect us as we go forward," Blake said. "I need to give Nick a call as soon as this meeting is over. I have a lot of new questions."

Harlan shook his head slowly. "Most of us don't need to get into that crap, especially now. Blake and Nick can just plan to give us their recommendations for things we need to do."

Paul laughed. So did everyone else.

"Do you think the Russian chess masters are still involved in the strategy and planning?" Blake asked.

"We know for sure they're still involved in a lot of aspects of this situation." Paul said. "Between the FBI and CIA, we've continued to compile quite a fact book on this. We'll plan to discuss any appropriate technical details as we go forward."

"Is there any evidence they have a quantum computer up in that area around Finland?" Colt asked.

"We don't know for sure yet, but we think they do. We think they plan to use it to fine tune the guidance systems for the Poseidon Missiles like they did in Jamaica," Paul said. "Having it on site up there in the area around Finland is an advantage in several ways. That's probably a good location to launch their cyber attacks from and it could be the origin of this current virus in the Federal Reserve System we've just referenced."

Colt grunted. "So, if our taskforce can shut down the quantum computer up there, we're going to solve a lot of different problems."

"Right," Paul said. "We'll eliminate a lot of new threats to our monetary system and also shut down any fine tuning on the guidance system for the missiles."

"Do you think the Russians developed this virus on their own?" Harlan asked.

"The Chinese are still the prime suspects for

developing the computer bug." Paul said. He scanned the faces around the table. "We think they're still working closely with the Russians."

"How big a group do you have working on this computer stuff?" Linda asked, giving Paul a curious glance.

"We have fifteen people in McLean working on this," Paul said. "The FBI also has a group in their Washington DC office working on this. The two groups have meetings everyday to discuss the technical details."

There was a brief silence.

Paul looked at Blake. "Do you have any recommendations for me at this time?"

"None other than to just keep talking to Nick," Blake said. "Linear regression and ordinary least squares regression are both parametric. The functions are defined in terms of a finite number of unknown parameters that are estimated from the data. Nick will understand that we need to use something much more robust and will be able to make some good recommendations on things we can do."

Paul nodded slowly.

"This is all bullshit to me," Harlan said. "I don't want to hear any more of these types of details."

Jim gave a slight grin and didn't comment.

"Bear with me for another minute," Paul said. "I have a valid objective here and there's something I want to clarify."

Harlan grunted and gave a slight shrug.

Paul looked directly at Blake. "Nick tells us the performance of regression analysis methods in practice depends on the form of the data-generation process used. He keeps emphasizing the performance depends on the quality of the assumptions made."

"In most cases the assumptions are testable," Blake said. "We've accumulated a large database at Boswic. I think Nick and I can make fast progress on validating any conclusions we come to."

Linda started to say something just as Paul's phone rang.

"It's Charles," Paul said, glancing at the caller ID which displayed the name of the CIA Director. He answered.

After a short conversation, Paul disconnected and looked at Colt. "Charles just talked with NSA. From what we can determine from the satellite images, the Russians are moving fast. It looks like they already have a structure in place to launch the missiles."

"Are any missiles in the images?" Colt asked.

"None have been spotted yet," Paul said, "however, based on all the information we have, we expect to spot them soon."

"And these new Poseidon Missiles are 80 feet long and 8 feet wide, right?" Linda asked.

"Right," Paul said. "We should have a good chance of spotting them when they arrive."

Harlan narrowed his eyes. "We know these bastards all want to bring us down as soon as they can and they're probably aware we're sending a taskforce up there. It's no surprise they're moving things along as fast as they can."

Paul nodded. "And that's why I referenced all the technical stuff. We can't let Russian and Chinese scientists outsmart us in any of the various areas we're getting into. We must at least keep up with them. Maybe we can even get one step in front."

"I can agree with your objective," Harlan said, "even if I don't want to hear much about all this mathematical crap."

Jim, Colt, and Linda all gave a knowing smile.

Blake showed no expression.

Paul stood. "Well, let's get moving. It now looks like we have no time to spare." He turned toward the doorway.

"I'll stay in close touch," Paul said as he made his exit.

Harlan looked at Grant. "You've been strangely quiet

through all this."

"I didn't find it necessary to say anything," Grant said. He looked at Harlan and grinned. "I agree with your comments on all the math stuff, but we all know it's an integral part of what we're dealing with now." He gestured toward Blake. "I'm glad we have experts dealing with all that."

Blake gave a thumbs-up. "These new Russian Poseidon Missiles are rumored to have the most sophisticated technology available. The more we know about them the better chance we'll have to shut them down in some way. If they get launched, they'll have no trouble hitting strategic spots in our country along any of our coastlines."

"The best way to cope with them is to prevent them from being launched," Colt said. He glanced at Linda. "We need to get on our way real soon."

Linda nodded.

"As we did in Jamaica, we're getting a couple of SEALIONs and a couple of Mark VI patrol boats complete with pilots on loan from the Navy," Harlan said.

"From what aircraft carrier?" Colt asked.

"I was told whichever one was closest to the area at the time," Harlan said.

"Will they be available immediately when we arrive?" Linda asked.

"Yes," Harlan said, "and, like before, they'll be the latest versions." He gestured to Blake. "Refresh our memories."

"The 90-foot SEALION III was designed to be heavily armed and to transport ten-man SEAL teams in shallow water at high speeds," Blake said. "They can reach speeds of around 80 knots. That's over 90 miles per hour. The Mark VI only reaches a speed of 40 miles per hour, but it's heavily armed, carries a crew of ten and will be perfect for maneuvering around all the islands in the archipelago and inspecting the shorelines."

"Will we contact the pilots in the same way we did in Jamaica?" Colt asked.

Harlan nodded. "I'll give you all the contact information before the taskforce leaves to go up there. As before, your mission is critical. There's no way the President wants any of those Poseidon Missiles to get launched and hit any of their targets."

Jim looked at Grant and leaned forward. "And our taskforce still consists of only Colt, Linda, FBI agents, and CIA agents?"

"Right," Grant said. "Whichever set of boats the taskforce uses at any given time, Colt, Linda and eight FBI agents will be in one of the boats and Mack Thomson and nine other CIA agents will be in the other boat. As before, Colt will command the taskforce. The pilots will stay with the boats and plan to do no fighting except in self defense."

Jim gave a slow nod. "We at Boswic will again earn our money and, along with the FBI and CIA, do all the initial fighting. However, we have tremendous backup from the Military if we get into big trouble and need it."

Chapter 19

The next morning on his private island near Finland, Ivan rose from his desk chair and walked over to a table in his office. He grabbed a large ceramic mug and filled it with the hot liquid from the fresh pot of coffee he had just brewed.

After again settling in his desk chair, Ivan savored the aroma of the coffee for a moment before he took a sip. He knew his next actions would be critical to the success of his new project and he wanted to do some heavy thinking, smart thinking to be exact.

His bosses, Lev and Yuri, were now making all the big strategic decisions, but he and Sergei still had the responsibility of developing all the tactical details and insuring everything happened correctly.

Ivan knew Lev and Yuri were taking orders from people even higher up in the Kremlin. There was a chain of decision making that had to be correct for the new project to succeed. If Project Neptune didn't succeed, he knew who would be blamed.

He had mixed feelings though. He felt great pressure, but in some ways he felt very grateful that he and Sergei were being given a second chance after their failure in Jamaica. He clinched a fist. They had to succeed this time.

Ivan took a deep breath and exhaled slowly. He then took a long slow drink of coffee. He was ready to go.

Sergei, Dmitri, and Pavel would join him in a few minutes. In a couple of hours, the four of them would meet with the Chinese contingent and begin reviewing all the technical details they would need to know to successfully complete their mission.

The United States must be defeated.

China had recently failed in their attempt to bring down the United States with germ warfare. Then Russia stepped in and tried to succeed with more conventional means, if you considered the Poseidon Missiles conventional, that is. That too failed.

Maybe Jamaica wasn't the best location for The Poseidon Initiative, Ivan thought. He shrugged. At least they had a chance to try again. Perhaps operating from this more northern location would work to succeed with Project Neptune.

Ivan took a slow sip of coffee. There was a lot to consider.

He, Sergei, Dmitri, and Pavel spent many hours yesterday studying the more complex issues represented in the massive amount of information in his primary computer file.

Everything was ready for him and his expanded group to begin finalizing the specific tactics for their next big initiative. They had received the broad strategy from Lev and Yuri, which Ivan figured had come from several other powerful people high up in the Kremlin. But he knew his group would again be solely responsible for the execution.

He was grateful he and Sergei weren't executed after their failure in Jamaica. He mentally shrugged. Apparently the Kremlin thought they were still useful. He knew this time they must not fail.

Ivan had found no glitches in the current plan to drain billions of dollars from the Federal Reserve System, and then destroy two significant areas in the United States with the Poseidon Missiles. He took another long slow drink of coffee and stared at a picture of the Marriner S. Eccles Federal Reserve Board Building in Washington DC.

Marriner S. Eccles had been Chairman of the Federal Reserve in times past. Franklin Delano Roosevelt had dedicated the building on October 20, 1937.

The American law enforcement and the people in charge of the current American financial structure would this time for sure get what they deserved. Ivan clinched s fist. Determination showed on his face.

Ivan glanced at two different lists of the twelve Federal Reserve Districts and smiled. There were twenty four Federal Reserve Branch banks on one list and twenty five on another list.

That was okay. Taking advantage of some inconsistencies could be a good thing.

Detroit, Michigan was shown on both lists as a branch of the Chicago District. Des Moines, Iowa was shown as a branch of the Chicago District on one list and not on the other. No problem for us, Ivan thought.

Ivan rechecked his notes on the functions of a central bank. In the United States, the central banking system was the Federal Reserve System. He smiled. There were some subtle differences between the classic global view of a central bank and the Federal Reserve System.

He planned to take advantage of some of those differences as they pertained to the International Monetary Fund (IMF). There were numerous loopholes he would exploit. He still had the necessary computer power available, and he was rechecking everything to make sure he took full advantage of his capability.

The Federal Reserve's Economic Value Model would play right into his hands. Game theory and the quantum computer were the main tools he needed. He knew Dmitri and Pavel would use specific financial formulas implemented at precise times to remain undetected for as long as possible.

If their actions were somehow detected by the Americans, he would ensure his team immediately applied all the necessary defenses they had already prepared.

Even if they were detected, Ivan felt they probably would have already extracted a sufficient amount of money. Most, if not all, of their monetary goals would still have been met.

Gaining enormous wealth was still his main goal and he didn't want to be totally dependent on Russia gaining more world-power for him to do that. If they took over the world, fine. He felt he would be in a favored position. If not, then he would at least be super wealthy and he would find a safe hideaway before it was too late.

Hearing a slight noise, Ivan looked toward the doorway. Sergei, Pavel, and Dmitri entered the room. He waited for them to settle into three of the empty chairs at his round conference table with seating for eight. Ivan moved over and joined them.

"Are the Chinese here yet?" Pavel asked.

"They should be here within a few more minutes," Ivan said. "They should be ready to immediately begin discussions on fine-tuning the guidance systems on the Poseidon Missiles."

Both Dmitri and Pavel nodded.

"We won't get into all the details here in the conference room, will we?" Sergei asked.

Ivan gave a short laugh and said, "I'll make sure we discuss just enough so the two of us will know the big picture about what's involved." He looked directly at Sergei. "As all this progresses, that will be a good thing for you and me to be knowledgeable about."

Sergei nodded and made no comment.

Ivan scanned the faces around the table. "Lev called about an hour ago. He wants us to move as fast as possible. Our moles have reported the Americans already know a lot about what we're doing here."

"Do they know we're planning to launch two 100 megaton Poseidon Missiles?" Pavel asked.

"Lev reported our moles think they do," Ivan said. "That's why Lev is emphasizing speed is of the essence."

"Are the Americans sending another taskforce?" Dmitri asked.

"Based on what the moles are telling us, that's a certainty," Ivan said.

A brief silence ensued.

"Do we plan to put any additional defensive measures in place around the islands?" Dmitri asked.

"Of course," Ivan said. "Moscow is supplying some of our newest and fastest small attack boats to patrol the waters around us. Using them will help us ward off any surprise attacks from the ocean or at least enable us to be more aware of what's going on out there."

Everyone gave a slow nod, but no one commented. Everyone seemed to be waiting for Ivan to continue.

"We'll also try to deploy our new group of assassins to the areas where they can be the most help," Ivan said, "especially our three best ones, Roman, Yan, and Eduard."

Pavel started to comment but stopped as Chung Ming and Fu Wong were escorted into the room. They immediately settled into two of the empty chairs at the table.

"We're here to help launch the missiles so they can destroy their targets," Chung said with narrowed eyes. His grin stretched wide on his face. "The United States will suffer great damage and they will never recover."

Fu leaned forward. "We will ensure the Poseidon

Missiles hit the right locations in the United States. I helped develop the guidance system they use, and I'm fully prepared to make any necessary fine-tuning adjustments."

"Do you think we'll have some fine-tuning issues?" Ivan asked.

Fu nodded. "There always are some improvements that could be made. I'm expert at identifying any last-minute adjustments that might be required."

"Our engineers originally developed the guidance system," Pavel said, "and thoroughly tested it. I was personally involved in a lot of the development and the testing."

Fu pursed his lips and gave a sow nod. "However, we improved it." He then displayed a wide grin. "We should make a good team."

Pavel didn't comment.

Chung leaned forward and stared at Ivan. "We're here to help us make certain we do the necessary damage to America. My bosses want to ensure that happens. I'm also one of China's leading experts on our improved guidance system for the missiles, and I'm real good at my job."

"You and your bosses failed on your germ warfare attempt a few years ago," Ivan said. "You failed to really do any permanent damage to the United States then and your cohorts didn't offer enough support for us to succeed in Jamaica. I hope you can help us do a lot better this time." He leaned toward Chung and returned his stare.

"There were some unfortunate incidents both times that ruined our plans." Chung narrowed his eyes. "We're all smarter now and we plan to help you succeed in bringing America down this time. Again, that's why Fu and I are here. We're providing some additional insurance."

Ivan regarded Chung carefully for a few moments and then gave a slow nod.

Sergei, Dmitri, and Pavel all stared at Chung, but none of them made any comments.

"And again, Fu and I are good at our jobs," Chung said. "Fu and I will make sure we inflict permanent damage on the United States this time."

"Okay, I hope that turns out to be the case." Ivan narrowed his eyes as he kept his gaze on Chung.

"There's no way the American way of life will survive our attacks from two one-hundred-megaton Poseidon Missiles," Fu said. He grinned and turned fully toward Chung.

"That's correct." Chung's face again stretched into a wide grin.

Ivan scanned the faces around the table and then said, "Okay, we'll go ahead and get started with our discussion." He paused. "And we'll ensure there are no screw ups this time."

Everyone nodded.

Chapter 20

At Boswic, Jim stopped in front of the desk in Harlan's office. Harlan looked up from what he was doing.

"Just wanted to stop for a few minutes and talk a couple of things over. Do you have time?" Jim asked.

"As long as we don't take more than half an hour," Harlan said. He gestured for Jim to sit down.

Jim plopped down in the closest chair.

"You worried about something?" Harlan asked

"I'm worried about a lot of things," Jim said. "I thought it would be useful to review some things before Colt and Linda fly up to Andrews."

Harlan narrowed his eyes and asked, "What's on your mind?"

"Blake just went over some more things with me, and he covered a lot of technical details about this new crop of Poseidon Missiles."

"Such as?"

"The new guidance system for one thing," Jim said. "The new missiles are much more sophisticated."

"You're referring to all this computer stuff that I'm

depending on you and Blake to keep up with?"

Jin nodded. "The new Russian Poseidon Missiles are rumored to have the most sophisticated technology available and remember each of the new one have a 100-megaton warhead."

"What's your point?"

"If any of the missiles get launched, we'll have a huge amount of destruction." Jim looked directly at Harlan. "We can't allow that. We must make sure we do all the right things to succeed."

Harlan shrugged. "We did that in Jamaica and we're in the process of doing that now. We're getting good support from the Navy and, like before, they'll be ready to step in if we have any major problems."

"I can't help thinking about 100-megatons being one tremendous destructive force."

"So that's what's bothering you right now?"

Jim hesitated for a moment and then nodded slowly.

"Remember the explosive force of the Poseidon Missiles we prevented from being launched in Jamaica were all 5 megatons. That's quite a blast too," Harlan said. "To put that in perspective, the bombs we dropped on Japan in World War II were much less than that. If I remember correctly, the bomb we dropped on Hiroshima was 1.5 megatons and the one we dropped on Nagasaki was 2 megatons."

Jim nodded.

"And, by the way, the experts inspecting those three Poseidon Missiles we captured have verified the warheads were all 5 megatons."

Jim gestured with both palms up. "Okay, you've made your point. Now we must do it again and prevent any future launches."

"The fact that we again have a couple of SEALIONs and a couple of Mark VI patrol boats complete with pilots will be a big help."

"How soon will we have them?" Jim asked.

"They'll be waiting for Colt and the taskforce when they get to Finland," Harlan said. "And we're getting the most recent generation of Navy patrol boats and the latest stealth boats for transporting SEAL teams."

"I'm trying to remember the details about the boats. Do you still have them available?"

Harlan opened a desk drawer and pulled out a piece of paper. He started reading from it. "The 90-foot SEALION III was designed to be heavily armed and to transport ten-man SEAL teams in shallow water at high speeds. They can reach speeds of around 80 knots. That's over 90 miles per hour. The Mark VI only reaches a speed of 40 miles per hour, but it's heavily armed, carries a crew of ten and will be perfect for scouting the shoreline around the island."

"I'm glad I stopped by," Jim said. "I'm feeling better about things. Sometimes you just need to talk to someone."

Harlan leaned forward. "And, like I told you, the boats will be in Finland and ready to use when Colt and the taskforce get there."

Chapter 21

Ivan Titov looked across the large table in his main conference room. The room was hi-tech and designed to support his upcoming activity. All his current team members were there to discuss and fine-tune their tactical plan for executing Project Neptune.

Sergei, Dmitri, Pavel, Roman, Yan, Eduard, Chung, and Fu all sat at the table with Ivan.

"We'll conduct all our meetings in English. We're all fluent in that language." Ivan's gaze took in both Chung and Fu. "Trying to mix Russian and Chinese can result in some big mistakes."

Everyone nodded.

Ivan looked directly at Chung. "Do you have the latest estimate as to when the missiles will arrive?"

"Beijing just informed me we have an unexpected problem," Chung said.

Ivan raised an eyebrow.

Chung leaned forward. "The ramjet engines haven't yet been able to create a bubble of gas for the missile to travel in. Friction with the water hasn't been reduced."

"The missiles are only traveling at 80 miles per hour right now," Fu said. "They won't arrive here for a few more days."

"Are they traveling at a depth of 3,280 feet where the ocean is deep enough?" Sergei asked.

Fu nodded. "80 miles an hour is still faster than the nuclear-powered attack submarines of the United States as well as their anti-ship missiles. And remember, each missile is powered by a miniature nuclear reactor, which effectively gives it unlimited range."

"We're confident the missiles will get here without being interfered with," Chung said. "It's just going to take longer." He looked at Ivan. "They'll take a little more than twice as long as we originally expected, but I think we can deal with that."

Ivan narrowed his eyes. "We should now expect Randall and his taskforce to arrive before they do. That's not good."

"You have a lot of defenses set up," Chung said. "You should be able to wipe out the taskforce as soon as they arrive. And your moles in Washington should be able to keep you informed on all the details about when the taskforce leaves and what their plan will be."

Ivan hesitated for a moment. A lot of thoughts were running through his mind. Should he continue the conversation or keep his thoughts to himself? He decided to continue the conversation. Maybe someone would have some brilliant suggestions.

"Don't forget Randall will be leading the taskforce and that hasn't worked out very well for us before." Ivan's gaze took in both Chung and Fu. "Do either of you have any good ideas about how we can improve our defense?"

"Have your moles informed you of when the taskforce

is leaving?" Chung asked.

"No," Ivan said, "I don't think that decision has been made yet." He leaned toward Chung. "Does that have any relevance to what defensive measures you might suggest?"

"The average depth of the water in the archipelago is only 78 feet," Chung said. "If Randall and the taskforce are surrounding the waterway leading into the launch area they might have some devices to detect the missiles coming in."

"Do you have a recommendation?" Ivan asked.

"Set up your defenses in a manner to keep the taskforce away from the area leading into the launch area," Chung said.

Fu nodded. "Start some big battles well away from here and try to keep the taskforce engaged until we've launched the missiles."

"Due to the ramjet problem, you're going to need some extra time to get everything working right before we launch, aren't you?" Ivan asked.

"I think we can fix that problem quickly, but we'll still have some fine-tuning to do with the technology we're supplying." Chung said. "We need to make sure everything is working perfectly in all circumstances before we launch. We must ensure the missiles hit their targets"

Ivan nodded slowly and then looked at Roman. "Do you have a good plan to knock Randall off before he comes over here?"

"I think it's good," Roman said, "and I'm confident I can execute it well. You can rest assured I can eliminate Randall."

Ivan stared at Roman for a few seconds. "Given the latest developments, I think we need to give it a try."

Roman flashed a big grin and waited for Ivan to continue.

"If we can eliminate Randall that will probably keep the taskforce from leaving the United Stated for a few days," Ivan said. "I've decided to let you give it a try."

Roman continued to grin and gave a thumbs-up.

Sergei looked at Ivan. "According to our moles, Linda Martinez, Randall's partner, is with him most of the time. I suggest you send someone with Roman since he probably won't be able to depend on Randall going anywhere alone. And we know Martinez is almost as good as Randall." Sergei gestured toward Roman. "He shouldn't have to face both of them by himself."

"I'm good enough to handle that," Roman said. "I'm the best gunman on the planet."

"Sergei has a good point," Ivan said. "It would be better if you had some help."

Roman narrowed his eyes and didn't comment.

Ivan looked at Yan. "Are you game?"

"Of course," Yan said. "The two of us can definitely handle this. Neither Randall nor Martinez will show up over here."

There was a brief silence.

"We have a fast jet, and it stays fueled up and ready to go." Ivan glanced at his watch. "How long will it take you to be ready to go?"

"We stay ready. Our bags are always packed," Roman said. He glanced at Yan.

Yan nodded.

Ivan gave a dismissive gesture. "Grab your bags and head for the plane. We'll try to intercept Randall and Martinez before they leave. We'll let the pilots know while they're still over the Atlantic whether to land in the Washington DC area or in Tampa."

Roman and Yan both bounced to their feet and rushed out of the room.

As Ivan watched them leave, he reached for his ringing phone. He saw on the display that it was a call from one of their moles in the CIA.

Ivan answered and immediately asked, "What's up?"

"I have some new information and I'm calling to let

you know about it," the mole said.

"And that is?"

"We just found out the American taskforce will be delayed for another day before they leave the States." The mole gave a short laugh. "The Americans aren't the only ones who can intercept phone calls." The mole hesitated.

"Go on. What else do you need to tell me?" Ivan asked impatiently.

"Randall will be getting some help from the United States Navy. They're furnishing a couple of their newest SEALIONs and a couple of their Mark VI patrol boats for him to use around the islands in the archipelago."

"What's a SEALION?"

"A navy craft that can hold ten warriors and go 90 miles an hour on the water," the mole said. "Randall and his taskforce will have two of them to use for any of their assaults needing transports over water."

"Go on."

"I'm guessing Randall will use the Mark VI patrol boats for reconnaissance. He'll probably go all around the archipelago and look for any new structures built close to the water."

"Structures built to launch the underwater missiles?"

"Precisely," the mole said.

"We'll work on making our launch area as undetectable as possible."

"How can you do that?"

Ivan explained and then asked, "Do you have any more information or advice right now?"

"That's all I have at the moment. We shouldn't stay on the call very long. I'll be back in touch when necessary."

"Quickly, while you're on the line, do you know where Randall will be tomorrow morning?"

The mole said, "As far as we can tell, he's going to be in Tampa."

"Thanks, I'll let you go."

Ivan heard the mole disconnect and noticed the people remaining at the table were staring at him.

"I just got some interesting information," Ivan said. He leaned forward and explained.

"Remember, we have some hi-tech boats too," Fu said. "They're better than any of the American boats and better than any of your Russian boats too. I'll make sure we have a couple shipped to us immediately."

Ivan gave a slow nod and then asked. "How soon will we get them?"

"Tonight," Fu said. "Chung and I will have one of our military cargo jets fly them over. We'll be well prepared to cope with any taskforce that shows up."

Chung glanced at Fu and then punched some digits on his phone. After a short conversation, he disconnected.

"The plane carrying the boats will be on the way here in a few minutes," Chung said.

Ivan, Sergei, and Eduard each gave a thumbs-up.

Chapter 22

In the Kremlin, Lev and Yuri sat at the round conference table in Lev's hi-tech office.

Each man had a laptop on the table in front of him.

A small piece of paper was also on the table, and several large screens were attached to the wall.

Each screen showed an organized array of images.

Lev picked up the piece of paper in front of him, glanced at it for a few seconds, and then pointed to one of the wall-mounted monitors.

"According to this latest dispatch I received, those are all the locations Ivan and Sergei will be using in the archipelago."

"All five of them?" Yuri asked.

"Only one is for launching the missiles." Lev pointed to one of the images on the screen. "The other four play a part in his defense strategy."

"Isn't it about time we had another talk with them?" Yuri asked.

"We should probably let things unfold a little more before we get together for another discussion. We'll give them a call in a few minutes. I think we can accomplish all we need to right now over the phone," Lev said. "We could even do a video conference call if you prefer."

"Sometimes it's good to see their reactions up close and in person. You can't tell that much about how they really feel when you're not sitting across the table from them."

Lev pursed his lips and didn't comment. He knew Yuri had a point, but he was reluctant to travel out of Moscow right now.

"Are you worried about something?" Yuri asked.

"Not really. I just want to stay home until we see how things unfold. I don't want to have to deal with Randall personally."

"So, you are indeed worried about something."

"Randall has proven to be a guy who can give us a lot of surprises."

"He hasn't even left the United States yet."

"We don't know that for sure. They probably know we have moles in the CIA and Randall's group might be putting out some misinformation."

Yuri nodded slowly as his eyes narrowed.

Lev said, "Even though it has its limitations, we'll go ahead and give them a phone call. We at least need to pass along all the latest information our bosses have given us."

"I guess comparing notes over the phone will be better than nothing," Yuri said. "We need to stay closely coordinated in any way we can."

Lev reached for his phone and punched a digit. Within a few seconds, he heard Ivan answer.

"Are the missiles there yet?" Lev asked.

"No," Ivan said, "there's been a slight delay."

"Oh?"

Ivan went on to explain.

"Yuri and I didn't know that."

"Doesn't the Kremlin stay in close touch with all the Chinese leaders," Ivan asked.

Lev said, "I think sometimes the Chinese leaders don't tell our bosses things that would reflect badly on Chinese expertise." He shrugged. "And maybe in this case, the Chinese leaders didn't know."

"I need to ask Chung about that," Ivan replied. "He probably knows something about that."

*****

In the conference room in his office complex on his private island, Ivan turned fully toward Chung. "Don't your bosses know about the malfunction with the ramjets on the missiles?"

"We don't always tell them every little detail about an operation," Chung said. He gave a slight shrug.

"You didn't want your technicians to look bad to Beijing?" Ivan asked.

"Sometimes it's better to not tell the upper level in Beijing everything," Chung said. "Sometimes people get executed."

Ivan spoke back into his phone. "Well, I think we figured out the reason you didn't know about the missile delay."

"Yeah, I could hear your conversation," Lev replied. "Stay on the line. We have some more things to talk about."

"I'm listening."

"Yuri and I don't know how true it is, but one of our

moles called us and reported that Randall and his taskforce won't leave to come over here until tomorrow afternoon."

"A mole called and gave us that report too," Ivan said. "We've sent a couple of our best assassins over to eliminate Randall before he leaves. They should get over there tonight." He went on to explain the details.

"Once the missiles are launched they're virtually unstoppable, right?"

"Right," Ivan said. "In the deeper part of the ocean, they'll travel at a depth of 3,280 feet and, once we have everything working, achieve speeds in excess of 200 miles per hour."

"I want to know how soon the missiles can be launched. Be sure to keep me informed."

"I'm sure it will be soon. We have a lot of experts waiting to start work as soon as the missiles arrive," Ivan said. "Once we launch, we should have no trouble bringing down the United States."

"Are you launching both missiles in succession like we planned?"

"Yes," Ivan said. "Everything we planned will be done. Each missile will be programmed to hit its assigned target."

A brief silence ensued.

"If Randall and his taskforce somehow get to the launch site, we can't let them shut you down like they did in Jamaica," Lev said.

"I'm confident Roman and Yan will dispose of Randall before he leaves the United States."

"I hope you're right. Keep me posted."

Ivan heard Lev disconnect.

Chapter 23

The following afternoon in Tampa, Colt and Linda walked toward the private hanger that housed the Boswic corporate jet at Tampa International airport. The jet sat in front of the hanger and looked ready for takeoff.

Linda flashed a look of concern. "I have a bad feeling."

"About what?"

"Not sure, but I have a good sixth sense."

Colt and Linda stopped and scanned the area closely. Colt noted Linda appeared calm, but alert and ready. That reinforced his feeling they were a good team.

There was a brief silence.

"We're too much out in the open for one thing," Linda said. "We probably should start moving again and move on a little faster than before."

They both started walking at a fast pace toward the Boswic private jet.

"Worried about a sniper?" Colt asked.

"That's one possibility."

"It's supposed to be a secure area."

"Maybe, but let's hurry up and get to the jet," Linda said. She started walking faster.

Colt kept pace.

*****

Roman stood with Yan behind a large storage building close to the Boswic private hanger.

After turning fully toward Yan, Roman asked, "Are you about ready to have some real fun?"

Yan tilted his head slightly and displayed a puzzled expression as he looked back at Roman. "Are you referring to eliminating Randall?"

"I'm thinking about how we're going to do that."

"What do you have in mind?"

"Let's toy with them a bit," Roman said. "We're supposed to be the best in the world, and we don't need to take them by surprise. We can gun them down whenever we want to without taking any big risks. I want to enjoy chatting with them for a minute or two before we eliminate them."

"It would be safer to fire from cover."

"We could have brought rifles if we had wanted to do that. I thought we agreed we wanted to handle this like an old-fashioned gunfight."

Yan gave a slight shrug. "That was what you wanted. I didn't argue with you."

"Randall is recognized globally as one of the top guns on the planet, the top gun by some people. I want to beat him in a fair fight. I have a statement to make."

"What if he's better than we think?"

"He's not," Roman said. "I'm going to prove I'm the best and I'm going to enjoy every moment of it."

Yan nodded slowly.

"I want to see Randall's reactions when we confront him. I'm looking forward to that." Roman looked directly at Yan. "I'm positive he's not nearly as good as a lot of people think he is. I can assure you he's definitely not as good as we are."

"What about his partner, Martinez?"

"The book on her is that's she's good, but not as good as Randall. You shouldn't have any trouble with her."

Yan gave a thumbs-up.

A brief silence ensued.

"Check your pistol again and make sure you have a full magazine, and make sure the first round is chambered," Roman said. He pulled his Sig-Sauer P226 from the holster and made a quick inspection. "We definitely don't want any careless oversights."

Yan had the same type of pistol as Roman. He removed it from his holster and quickly went through the procedure. He again gave a thumbs-up.

Each man inserted his pistol back into his holster and gave it a couple of quick pats.

Within the next few seconds Roman heard the message come into his earpiece and then he looked at Yan. "They're coming this way. It's show time. You ready for action?"

"Did you just get a notice?"

"Yep, they're about 50 yards away and heading this direction."

After a quick nod, Yan took a deep breath and exhaled.

"Just what we were expecting, there are only the two of them, Randall and Martinez," Roman said. "Everything is going to plan. We should have no trouble on this mission. Especially since no one else on the planet can match our expertise with pistols." He grinned.

Yan also grinned

Roman motioned vigorously for Yan to come along as he turned and walked toward the nearest corner of the storage building.

"Let's go get 'em partner," Roman said as they rounded the corner. He flashed another big grin.

Yan returned the grin.

*****

Colt saw two large men come around a back corner of the nearby storage building. They walked straight toward him and Linda. He noticed the two Russian-looking men were wearing big grins and had expressions of recognition as they approached.

Each man had a pistol in a holster strapped to his right thigh.

"They look like they know who we are," Linda said.

Colt gave a short grunt. "I think you're right. Get ready."

Linda and Colt came to an abrupt halt and stood beside each other, prepared to take any necessary action.

The two men stopped about ten feet away and stood side by side. They both stared at Colt and remained silent.

Colt noted that each man was heavily muscled and carried his pistol in a fast-draw style holster.

"You seem to know who we are," Colt said.

Neither man made any comment.

One man stared at Colt.

The other man stared at Linda.

No fear showed in their eyes.

The man directly in front of Colt grinned and jiggled the fingers on his right hand.

The man in front of Linda did exactly the same thing.

"Of course we know who you are," the man in front of

Colt said. “That’s why we’re here. We know your schedule and your plans.” He continued to stare at Colt and flashed an even bigger grin.

“And that means?” Colt asked.

“That means you only have a few minutes to live,” the man standing in front of Colt said.

Colt could see they were enjoying the confrontation. He hoped they would get a little careless. He figured he had time to glance at Linda. She was concentrating on the man in front of her and appeared ready to react. He and Linda had been a team for over a year now. Colt was confident she would follow the plan they had used several times before. He looked quickly back at the large muscular man in front of him.

The man directly in front of Colt flashed an acid grin and spoke in a menacing heavily accented voice. “You’ve been messing around with the wrong people for a long time and that’s about to stop.”

“And who are those people?” Colt’s gaze took in both of the menacing figures. He noted both men were roughly the same size in every way, muscles and all.

Linda stayed silent.

The man in front of Colt narrowed his eyes. “We never reveal our clients. That’s unprofessional.”

“And we don’t like answering questions from dummies,” the man directly in front of Linda said. He narrowed his eyes and grinned at Colt for a few seconds before he looked back at Linda.

The two men continued to stare at Colt and Linda. No fear showed in their eyes.

Respecting Linda’s ability, Colt didn’t worry about the man in front of her. He kept his attention glued on the one directly in front of him.

“What’s your name?” Colt asked.

“Roman Arnold,” the man said with a grin. “You’ve probably heard of me. I have a big reputation.”

Colt gave a slight nod and gestured toward the man in front of Linda. "And your name is."

The man also grinned as he replied, "Yan Block is the name. You've probably heard of me too."

Neither Colt nor Linda made any comment.

Colt figured there was nothing to be gained by making any type of comment. He stayed on full alert and waited.

Roman glanced toward Yan and then looked back at Colt.

"Ok Randall," Roman said. "It's time we told you goodbye. Your time on earth has come to an end."

Roman's eyes narrowed as he drew his pistol.

Yan also drew his pistol.

With a fluid motion, Colt brushed back his coat with his right hand and removed his pistol from the holster positioned toward the back of his right hip. Executing a quick forward snap, he aimed and pulled the trigger of his Glock 19. The entire sequence had only taken half a second.

Roman dropped to the concrete.

Hearing another bang to his left, Colt glanced toward Yan. He was also on the concrete. A Sig-Sauer P226 pistol was on the concrete beside each body. Linda had taken care of her part of the confrontation.

Colt and Linda stepped forward to examine the bodies.

It was obvious the two men were dead.

Colt fished his secure satellite phone from a pocket and hit a button.

"Are you calling Grant?" Linda asked.

"Yeah, he'll mop up and take care of anything that needs attention," Colt said. "You call Jim and give our report."

Linda punched a digit on her phone.

After both finished their phone conversations, Linda turned toward Colt. "Good job partner." She grinned.

Colt returned the grin. "Looks like you're handling the

emotional side of this well."

"I was involved in many situations in the Marines that were a lot more gruesome," Linda said. "And I agree with your thinking: it's best to not get uptight."

Colt gave a thumbs-up.

"Jim told me he and Harlan will contact us during our flight from Andrews to Finland and make sure we're briefed on all the latest information," Linda said.

Colt nodded. "And any strategy discussions we need to have among our team we can do on the flight up."

As soon as the various law-enforcement personnel arrived, Colt and Linda again turned toward the Boswic private jet and were soon on their way to Andrews Air Force Base just outside Washington DC.

Chapter 24

In the office complex on his private island, Ivan Titov studied the six people sitting around the large table in his main conference room. The room was hi-tech and designed exclusively to support his next mission. All his immediate team currently in Finland were there for discussion. He needed to perfect their plan for executing Project Neptune.

Sergei, Dmitri, Pavel, Eduard, Chung, and Fu all sat around the table and were obviously waiting for him to begin the discussion.

Leaning toward Chung, Ivan asked, "How close are the missiles?"

"Our control center in Beijing tells me they're less than 500 miles away and should arrive here early tomorrow morning," Chung said.

Ivan narrowed his eyes and didn't comment.

Chung displayed a big grin and said, "All my new scientists are here and ready to start work. We'll have everything in top working order quickly, you'll see."

Ivan nodded slowly. "Okay, make sure Dmitri and Pavel are involved in any important discussions regarding the fixes for any of the problems."

Chung continued to grin. "We'll do that for sure."

Fu also grinned as he gave a thumbs-up.

"Make sure all the discussions are in English," Sergei said, "and remember we agreed to that earlier."

"A couple of my scientists have a little trouble with English." Chung looked directly at Sergei. "However, that's no big problem. Fu and I will translate for them."

Sergei and Ivan both narrowed their eyes and stared at Chung for a few seconds, but neither made a comment.

"Do you have a problem with that?" Chung asked.

"Since we don't speak Chinese, I don't think we have a choice," Ivan said. He started to say more just as he heard a distracting noise.

After glancing at his vibrating phone on the table, Ivan picked it up and answered. He listened for a few seconds without comment and then asked, "How did you hear about this?"

"My group stays informed about all the FBI reports," the mole at the other end of the line said.

"So, both of our top guns were eliminated?" Ivan asked.

"Yes," the mole said. "Both Randall and Martinez were too good for them. According to the FBI report our top guns each lost a fast draw contest." He went on to give more details.

"I knew Randall was good, but I didn't know Martinez was that good." Ivan hesitated for several seconds. "Our researchers need to do a better job going forward."

"I think you have an accurate point," the mole said. "I needed to give you the update. I must go now."

Ivan moved the phone away from his ear and stared at it for several seconds after he heard the mole disconnect.

Sergei looked at Ivan. "From what I heard you say that

was very bad news, right?"

"Right," Ivan said. He shook his head slowly. "Roman and Yan confronted Randall and Martinez and lost a fast draw contest?"

"Did Randall and Martinez have any help?" Eduard asked.

"Nope," Ivan said. "According to the report, it was a fair fight and our guys lost, plain and simple."

"If the time comes, I don't think I'll challenge Randall unless I have no other option." Eduard looked directly at Ivan. "Roman was a lot faster with a pistol than I am."

"Yeah," Ivan said. "No sense in dying needlessly." He pursed his lips and again shook his head slowly. "I guess we're going to have to fight Randall over here now."

A brief silence ensued.

Sergei looked at Ivan and motioned toward Eduard. "He's the only skilled assassin we have on our immediate staff now. We need at least one more. Eduard will probably need a partner on some upcoming assignments, and it will be best to have someone he's worked with a few times."

"The Kremlin has a good supply of talented assassins," Ivan said. "I'll call Lev and Yuri. They can probably help us out on this."

"Would you go ahead and do that now?" Eduard asked. He gestured with both palms up. "The sooner I start working with another assassin the better we'll be as a team when Randall shows up over here."

Ivan pushed a button on his phone that was still in his hand. He heard Lev answer.

"I'll get straight to the point," Ivan said. "We just lost Roman and Yan and we need another assassin."

"Did Randall and Martinez take them out?" Lev asked.

"Yes and without any help," Ivan said. "We knew Randall was real good, but now we know he's even better than we thought. It looks like Martinez is real good too."

Lev grunted. "We'll need to keep that in mind as we

go forward. China is continuing to offer to supply assassins to the Kremlin when we request them."

"Are they all monsters like the ones Randall eliminated in Jamaica?" Ivan asked.

"Yes and all have superior weapons skills too," Lev said. "They pose a good option to consider, and Beijing has offered to send the best one they have left to help us."

"Do you know his name?"

"Yang Woo"

"Hold on a minute."

Ivan looked at Eduard. "Have you ever heard of the Chinese assassin named Yang Woo?"

"No, and I don't want him as my partner no matter how good he is," Eduard said. "I want a Russian partner. There are too many things that can go wrong with the communication if I have a Chinese partner."

Ivan nodded and then spoke back into the phone. "Eduard wants a Russian partner."

"Yuri and I both think it's a good idea for Yang to come over and join your forces anyway. He can boost your defenses against Randall and his taskforce," Lev said. "Eduard doesn't have to partner with him."

"Are you going to send a Russian assassin over here too?"

"Have you ever heard of Taros Kats?"

"No," Ivan said. "Give me a couple of seconds and I'll ask Eduard."

Ivan looked at Eduard. "Do you know Taros Kats?"

"I've worked with him on a couple of dangerous assignments. He's real good. Are we going to get him?" Eduard asked.

Ivan spoke back into the phone. "Eduard has worked with him before and has a high opinion of him. Are you going to send Taros to join us?"

"Yes, he'll be there this afternoon" Lev said. "We need to make sure Randall is eliminated as quickly as possible after he gets to Finland. He'll be our priority, our main target. You need to brief Taros and make sure he knows eliminating Randall is his top priority."

"You can count on that," Ivan replied. "I probably want to get rid of Randall more than you do."

"Speaking of Randall, there's something else I need to tell you," Lev said. "Randall will use the Mark VI patrol boats to go all around the archipelago and look for any new structures you've built close to the water."

"Like anything to launch the underwater missiles, right?"

"Precisely," Lev said.

"We'll continue working on making everything as undetectable as possible," Ivan replied. "We'll ensure everything is undetectable from satellites as well as close inspection from the water."

"By using a lot of different camouflage techniques?"

"Yes, do you have any advice?"

"No, you know a lot more about your specific situation than I do," Lev said. "Good luck. I'll be back in touch when necessary."

Ivan heard Lev disconnect and noticed everyone around the table was staring at him.

"Two new assassins will be joining us," Ivan said. He leaned forward and explained.

Sergei narrowed his eyes. "We can definitely use Taros right away. He and Eduard can each command one of the two hi-tech patrol boats we have from China."

"We should have another chance to eliminate Randall and his group when they're in their boats patrolling the islands," Ivan said. He grinned. "And, unlike Jamaica, this time we'll have two boats instead of one."

Everyone gave a thumbs-up.

Ivan scanned the faces around the table and then leaned forward. "Okay, let's firm up our plans. We already know the first thing we need to get done is eliminate

Randall and his taskforce when they arrive tomorrow."

"Did any of the moles know what time they're arriving?" Sergei asked.

"They all think it will be around noon," Ivan said, "and according to the phone conversations we intercepted, they're going to use the Mark VI patrol boats immediately and make a full sweep around the islands in the archipelago."

"Looking for any of our facilities, right?" Chung asked.

"Right," Ivan said, "and as soon as Taros gets here, he and Eduard need to take our boats out around the archipelago and make notes of anything that looks suspicious. Then, if we can, we need to fix any problems we find as quickly as possible."

Everyone nodded.

"Now, since Randall and his taskforce of 20 will all be out in their two Mark VI patrol boats, give me some good ideas on how to eliminate them this time," Ivan said.

"We should have a good option immediately," Chung said, "With all the different islands we have a lot of hiding places for our boats. Let's ambush them and use the enhanced firepower on our super fast stealth boats to destroy his patrol boats when Randall is inspecting our area." He stared at Ivan. "Since we now have two boats, we have a lot better situation than you did in Jamaica."

Ivan looked around the table. "Anyone have any objections making that our first initiative?"

"Sounds good to me," Sergei said.

Everyone else nodded.

Ivan's glance took in both Chung and Fu. "Are either of you experts on how to operate this new version of your stealth boat?"

Chung gestured toward Fu. "Both of us are thoroughly trained on how to use every aspect of this new model."

"Okay," Ivan said. "We'll plan on each of you being

on board your selected boat when Taros arrives. He and Eduard will each command a boat and you can each be onboard a boat to advise the crew on what to do to operate all the equipment."

Chung and Fu both nodded and flashed a big grin.

"Okay," Ivan said. "We have a plan. I'll call one of our moles back later and see if he has any more details about Randall's schedule involving the Mark VI patrol boats and the SEALIONs."

Chapter 25

At the FBI headquarters in Tampa, Grant sat in his desk chair and waited for Steve Lockett to arrive from Washington and the Boswic leadership group to come over for a coordination meeting. There was a lot to discuss.

As before, the Kremlin and Beijing were staying in the background as another brilliant strategy continued to unfold. There was no doubt Russia and China had continued their quest to work together and bring down the United States of America.

Grant savored a swallow of coffee just as a call came through on his secure line. He glanced at the caller ID and answered.

"Has your meeting with Boswic started yet?" Ken asked.

"Nope, but they should be arriving in a few minutes."

"Good," Ken said. "Steve just landed and he's on his

way from the airport. He should be there in a few minutes too and he's already reviewed all the new data I just sent to you."

"I'll plan on him leading the discussion."

"The new data from RAND should be interesting to all of you. It contains some new detailed analysis on what Russia and China are doing."

"Does it have a lot of specifics regarding the missiles?"

"Quite a bit, including confirmation that there are two of them and they each have a 100-megaton warhead."

"Just how accurate is this latest information from RAND?" Grant asked.

"It's backed up by data from the CIA and from several other intelligence agencies," Ken said. "And there's another thing I should mention before you have your discussion."

Grant narrowed his eyes and waited.

"We're certain both Russia and China have new surveillance satellites in orbit?"

"Do you know how many?"

"Four more satellites we know of," Ken said, "You'll need to alert Randall he's going to be watched very closely. Also encourage him to ask for help as soon as he thinks he needs some. Due to the seriousness of this, all branches of the Military are staying ready to jump in, especially the Navy."

"The President has approved that?"

"Yes, and it's the same strategy as before."

"Let Randall handle it if he can?"

"That's correct," Ken said. "The President doesn't want to take a big chance on starting World War III, but he doesn't want two monster Poseidon Missiles to get launched toward the United States either. He's hoping Randall will come through like he's done before and this threat will be shut down."

"I'll give Colt the latest details as soon as he lands in

Finland and remind him the Military is standing by if he needs them. I'll continue to urge him to stay ready to ask for help and not take any extreme risks."

Ken gave a short laugh. "We already know you and Colt have different definitions of what an extreme risk is."

Grant also laughed. "Yeah that's very true."

"Have a good meeting," Ken said. "I'll keep you posted on any new developments." He disconnected.

Grant put down his phone and moved over to his round conference table with seating for six just as Harlan, Jim, and Blake were ushered into Grant's spacious office. The Boswic contingent settled into three of the empty chairs.

"Steve should be here in a few minutes." Grant gestured toward the coffee pot. "Help yourself if you want some. From what I just learned, you'll probably need it."

"What did you just learn?" Harlan asked.

"Let's wait until Steve gets here before we dig into all that," Grant said. He leaned forward. "However, I'll go ahead and tell you the Russians and Chinese have at least four new surveillance satellites in orbit. Everything our taskforce does out in the open in the Finland area will be under observation."

"We have surveillance satellites too. Have we learned any more about what the enemy is doing in the area around the western shore of Finland?" Harlan asked.

"Steve should have some information about that," Grant said. "He'll give us an update when he gets here. According to Ken, he's completed a lot of analysis on the latest data."

Harlan gestured toward Blake. "He's completed a lot of analysis on information compiled from older data. Steve and Blake can both provide a lot of new insights. Between the two of them, we should learn a few more things that can do us a lot of good."

Blake nodded. "I've identified several things that should be valuable to the taskforce."

At that point Steve walked into the office carrying a large folder. He put it down on the floor beside him as he eased into a chair next to Grant at the round conference table.

"Can you use some coffee?" Grant asked.

Steve grunted. "Thanks, but I drank a lot more on the flight down than I need."

"Then let's get straight to business," Grant said. He glanced at Steve. "Give us the new information you have."

Steve opened the large folder on the floor beside his chair. He took a moment to scan some of the contents.

"A lot of camouflage coverings have been constructed in numerous areas around various islands," Steve said. "That's obviously to shield some newly constructed areas from being spotted by our satellites. I've alerted all the people who control the satellites and all who analyze the data. They know what to stay alert for."

"Will they immediately keep us informed on what's going on?" Harlan asked.

"Yes," Steve said. "They'll instantly alert Grant and me about anything significant and we'll make sure everyone stays up to date on what's happening up there."

Harlan nodded.

Steve looked at Blake. "We've compared notes on a lot of information in the last few days. It will probably be a good idea to share a lot of it while we're all together. Go ahead and start us off."

"Of course our main concern is to keep Russia from launching any of the new Chinese-enhanced Poseidon Missiles," Blake said. He scanned the faces around the table. "Steve and I have completed a lot of research on them, and the new models look more deadly than we originally thought. It looks like the 100-megaton warheads have been perfected." He went on to explain.

Harlan narrowed his eyes and winced but didn't comment.

"Besides killing a lot of people and destroying a lot of infrastructure, the new versions could be super effective in instantly disabling many of our critical functions, and eventually our entire economy," Steve said.

Blake nodded. "That's a fact."

"We already knew they're nuclear-powered and they're designed to cross entire oceans to reach their targets," Steve said. "They can be launched from devices constructed on the ocean or they can be carried by specially designed submarines. We know what their launching scheme was in Jamaica, now we must figure out exactly what they're planning to do in Finland."

Blake nodded. "And remember, as they're crossing the Atlantic Ocean, the missiles can travel at depths far below what any submarine can reach, even our best nuclear subs."

"Are we absolutely sure the strength of the warhead is 100 megatons?" Harlan asked.

"Yes," Steve said. "You heard Blake's explanation. Just to put that in perspective, the bomb we dropped on Hiroshima in World War II was 1.5 megatons and the one we dropped on Nagasaki was 2 megatons."

Harlan grunted. "We better make sure none of those damned missiles ever get launched."

Everyone nodded.

Grant looked at Harlan and gave a short laugh. "I'd say that's the understatement of the year."

"But it's the damned truth," Harlan said, "and we'd better keep that in mind. We must succeed in doing that like we did in Jamaica."

Grant leaned forward. "I think our President has an even greater sense of urgency this time. If Colt and the taskforce have any big problems, I'm sure our Military, especially our Navy, will be immediately unleashed." He gestured toward Harlan. "We all agree with what you just mentioned."

A brief silence ensued.

"We know the Poseidon Missiles can normally travel underwater at a speed of 80 miles an hour," Steve said. "Even that is faster than our nuclear-powered attack submarines as well as their anti-ship missiles. And if they fix their ramjet engines to create a bubble of gas for the missile to travel in and reduce the friction with the water, don't forget the missiles will be able to travel at a speed of 200 miles per hour."

Blake nodded. "And don't forget these missiles will be able to travel at a depth of 3,280 feet, which, again, is far lower than any of our submarines can go. It's definitely a Tsunami Apocalypse Torpedo powered by a miniature nuclear reactor which gives unlimited range."

"Do we know if Tampa and Washington DC are still their main targets?" Jim asked.

"That's the last information we have," Steve said. "NSA is still intercepting many of their phone calls and they're still able to decrypt most of the conversations. We're likely staying well informed on that subject."

Harlan narrowed his eyes and then pressed his right palm to his forehead. "We damned sure better succeed up there in Finland."

"I don't think we all could agree more on that," Grant said. He looked directly at Harlan. "There's no doubt we'll for sure give this next mission our best effort."

Steve thumbed through the folder beside him and removed a single sheet of paper. He glanced at the paper for a moment and then scanned the faces of the people sitting around the table. "I've mentioned this before, but I think I should remind you of the details before we go to another subject."

No one commented. Everyone kept their gaze on Steve.

"The United States did some testing relating to underwater nuclear explosions back in the 1940's and 50's," Steve said. "They named two of the projects

Crossroads Baker and Hardtack I Wahoo. The bombs detonated were roughly the sizes of the ones dropped on Hiroshima and Nagasaki. The explosions ejected seawater more than a mile high and caused considerable damage around the area." He looked at the faces around the table. "Some old warships staged in the general area were vaporized. Others further away were tossed into the air for miles. All were heavily damaged with crushed or cracked hulls."

There was a brief silence.

Harlan looked at Steve and gave a thumbs-up. "It's good you reminded us of that. It's sobering."

"Well, I guess we now have an even better understanding of the threat we're facing," Grant said. "And we know we must stop it. Let's see if there's anything more we need to do to help Colt and the taskforce."

"When they arrive in Finland, they'll quickly board the two Mark VI patrol boats and scout all the islands in the Archipelago, right?" Jim asked.

"Right," Grant said. "And we'll remind them that both Russian and Chinese surveillance satellites will be zeroed in on where they are and what they're doing."

"Think the enemy will try to stop them from scouting the islands?" Harlan asked.

"Probably," Grant said. "Our satellites have spotted a couple of boats like the one they had in Jamaica being delivered there."

"Do we have any more information about that?" Jim asked.

Grant gestured to Steve.

"We know the Chinese have more small hi-tech boats like the one called the Sea Ghost they had in Jamaica," Steve said. "The satellite photos show those that were delivered to the island in the archipelago have the same look. Remember they have some technological aspects that give them a lot of advanced stealth characteristics and we know they're super fast."

"How fast is the one we captured in Jamaica?" Jim asked.

"It has reached a speed of 110 miles per hour in our testing," Steve said as his eyes narrowed.

Harlan slapped his forehead again with his right palm. "How can the Chinese be that advanced?"

"The Chinese seem to concentrate on developing hi-tech weapons more than we do," Steve said. "They certainly throw a lot more funding at it than we do."

"Are we doing the testing of the captured boat down there in the waters around Guantanamo?" Jim asked.

Steve nodded. "Yes and that's also where we took the three older Poseidon Missiles we captured. We have a complex there we're using for all our inspections."

"I just to doublecheck. What size are the warheads on the three captured missiles we've been inspecting?" Harlan asked.

"They were all 5 megatons," Steve said. "Remembering the statistics I just gave you about the two atom bombs we dropped on Japan, these three missiles could also have done a lot of damage if they had ever been launched."

Harlan clinched his right fist and shook his head slowly. "Thank God we succeeded down there in Jamaica. Now we must do it again."

Everyone nodded.

Chapter 26

Late morning the next day, two Mark VI patrol boats entered the ocean from a private dock in a secluded area on the western shore of Finland.

Colt and Linda rode with a pilot and eight FBI agents in the first boat. Mack Thomson rode with a pilot and nine other CIA agents in the second boat.

Under camouflage fatigues, each warrior wore a suit of tungsten disulfide-based nano-composite material, over five times stronger than steel. The short-sleeved armor suits protected each person from neck to knee.

Colt, Linda, and each FBI agent carried a SIG 556 rifle and a Glock 19 pistol. The Glocks had 15-round magazines filled with 9mm ammunition. The SIGs had a short stock and two pistol grips. The magazine could hold 30 NATO 5.56mm rounds. Each rifle weighed 7.8 pounds, was 37 inches long, and could fire 900 rounds per minute.

Each CIA agent carried an M16A2 rifle, using NATO 5.56mm ammunition, and a Browning HP 9mm pistol.

Each rifle magazine held 30 rounds, and each pistol magazine held 13 rounds.

Everyone had extra magazines for a sustained firefight, if necessary.

Sleek and low in the water, the Mark VI patrol boats moved forward at 40 miles per hour without making much noise.

The pilot glanced at Colt. "This craft is better than the older model, the Mark V. Haven't studied all the statistics yet, but I can tell a big difference." He swept a hand down the length of the boat. "The boat is 84.8 feet long and it can carry eight additional people in addition to a crew of ten." He paused. "You probably noticed we have six mounted 50 caliber machine guns."

"We used this boat in Jamaica," Colt said. "Our taskforce is the same one we had there." Colt grinned. "We're all familiar with a Mark VI patrol boat."

The pilot returned the grin and gave a dismissive wave. "We'll keep touring various locations in the archipelago. Let me know if you decide on any specific routes while we're out here."

"You choose the routes," Colt said. "On this trip we just want to make a general inspection."

The pilot nodded.

Colt looked at Linda. "Go ahead and start scanning."

Linda flipped a switch on the device in her hand and pointed it toward the nearest island.

A small green light blinked on top of the device. It was designed to turn red if any nuclear material was detected within 500 yards and yellow if certain types of drugs were detected.

Colt still didn't know how the device worked, but they had used it successfully in Jamaica. He glanced at the blinking green light and then scanned the area.

No other boats were near them.

Colt removed his secure satellite phone from a pocket

and punched a button. In about a second, he heard Mack answer.

"Have you checked with any of your bosses at the CIA?" Colt asked.

Mack gave a short laugh. "No, I was waiting to hear from you. So, what's our plan?"

"We'll just make a general inspection of the area," Colt said. "Our boat will lead the way, and our pilot will choose the routes. Follow along and keep an eye out for anything we want to make note of."

"Roger."

"Since Grant has again been designated as my primary contact throughout this mission, I'll call him and see if he has the latest satellite updates," Colt said. "You should call your bosses at the CIA and discuss any new information they have. We'll compare notes when we've finished our conversations."

"Roger, talk to you in a bit."

Colt heard Mack disconnect. He looked at the pilot and said, "When we get close to the shore of any of the islands slow to 15 miles per hour until we've completed our inspection."

The pilot nodded.

Colt punched a button on his phone, and he heard Grant answer.

"Do you have any of our satellite updates?" Colt asked.

"Just got them," Grant said. "There are no enemy patrol boats out on the water yet. They're probably still docked in an area hidden by some kind of camouflaged top."

Colt gave a short laugh. "Yeah, that's to be expected. Good thing Ivan Titov can't camouflage the whole archipelago."

Grant laughed too and then said, "I'll call you as soon as we spot them on the water."

"Do you have any new information about anything else?" Colt asked.

"No, Grant said. "I've kept you completely up to date and I'll continue to do so."

"Thanks. I'll talk to you later." Colt disconnected.

*****

Eduard Sidorov stood on the deck of the first hi-tech boat that had been provided by China. They were still docked in Ivan Titov's secure harbor about 100 yards from his headquarters building.

The second hi-tech boat was still docked there too. It was about 20 yards away and Eduard could see Taros standing on the deck of it.

Eduard spoke into his tactical communications microphone, and he heard Taros answer immediately.

"Are you ready to go after them?" Eduard asked.

"They're out there on the water?"

"Yep," Eduard said, "and, just as we expected, they're in two Mark VI patrol boats."

"Let's go. We'll follow you."

Eduard saw Taros give a thumbs-up..

Glancing toward Chung Ming, Eduard asked, "Are you sure this baby can outrun any American craft?"

"I'm positive," Chung said. "We should be able to make sharp turns at 110 miles an hour without turning over."

"Have you been personally involved in the testing?"

"Yes, but I've never been going over 90 when I made any sharp turns. I had no problems, but I didn't want to push my luck," Chung replied. "Some of the test engineers told me they had made sharp turns at 110 miles per hour." Chung gave a slight shrug. "I've never felt the urge or the need to try that."

"Maybe we should do that just to know what our options are if we need to get out of an area in a hurry," Eduard said.

"I don't think we should try that now. It won't be a good thing if we turn over and being able to make a sharp turn at 90 miles an hour should be good enough to get us out of any predicament we get into." Chung looked directly at Eduard. "I think we need to get moving and eliminate the American taskforce as soon as we can."

Eduard nodded and checked his watch. He fished his secure satellite phone out of his pocket and punched a digit.

"We're moving out," Eduard spoke into his phone.

"Randall and his taskforce are only a few miles from you," Sergei said. "Both their boats are staying relatively close together. It looks like they plan to stay within about 30 yards of each other. Our satellites are zeroed in on them. We'll monitor the situation and keep you advised as is necessary."

"I'll be back in touch in a few minutes." Eduard disconnected from his call as his boat moved out into deeper water.

Two boats about a mile away were coming in his direction. He raised his binoculars and studied them. They were both Mark VI patrol boats. It had to be Randall and the American taskforce."

With all of his men being highly trained professionals, Eduard knew it wasn't necessary to give a lecture on elementary items, but it would feel good. That was why he would do it, because it would feel good, damned good. He gave a one-minute lecture and let off a lot of steam as his boat continued into the open water. He felt better now about confronting Randall.

Eduard knew the two boats he and Taros commanded would be hard to detect. Each boat sat low in the water and used navigation equipment developed by top engineers.

Their improved stealth design and camouflage-like coloring was designed for blending with the water and being almost invisible. Having enormous funding offered huge advantages.

This was what he lived for, Eduard thought. He grinned. Each of the two stealth boats had enough firepower to wreak havoc on the Mark VI patrol boats. They would sink them immediately.

If Colt Randall was on one of the boats coming toward him, Randall would get what he deserved. His time on this planet would be over.

Chapter 27

In McLean, Virginia, Paul Collins, head of the Terrorist Threat Investigation Unit, hurried into his boss's corner office at CIA headquarters.

"Mack just called. They've started inspecting the islands in the archipelago," Paul said.

"How many have they checked?" Charles asked.

"They're just starting," Paul said. "They've slowed to 15 miles per hour. Everything is in progress and going according to plan."

"Hopefully they can find the location of the missile launch site fairly quickly."

Paul nodded and then narrowed his eyes. "So far, our analysts haven't been able to tie everything completely together. The details we've uncovered have been too scattered. We suspect Ivan Titov will have the launch equipment set up on the island his headquarters is on, but we don't know that for sure. Hopefully we can confirm that quickly."

"Yeah," Charles said. "We need to get more clarity on exactly what's going on up there in that archipelago as quickly as possible. Maybe we'll tie some more of the details together today."

*****

Ivan sat in the main conference room in his headquarters in the archipelago and scanned the faces around the large table. Sergei, Pavel, Dmitri, and Yang were present.

Yang narrowed his eyes and looked at Ivan. "We have the superior boats. We should try to eliminate Randall's whole crew immediately."

Ivan punched a button on his secure satellite phone. He heard Eduard answer.

"Are you out of the harbor yet?" Ivan asked.

"Yes," Eduard said, "and we got lucky, the two Mark VI boats are coming in our direction."

"Have they spotted you?"

Eduard said, "It's unlikely. They haven't increased their speed to come after us."

Ivan grunted. "All the stealth characteristics must be working well."

Eduard didn't comment.

"Our satellite pictures confirm the boats are carrying the taskforce we've been expecting." Ivan hesitated for a moment. "And Colt Randall is on the deck of the lead boat. You need to eliminate him and the whole taskforce right now."

"We definitely will," Eduard said. "We're in the process of getting into a better position."

"Do you have the torpedoes ready to fire?"

"Yes," Eduard said, "all four of them. We'll aim two at each boat and stagger the firing by ten seconds so the torpedoes won't be too close together. We want to eliminate the possibility that Randall can destroy more than one of them with a single defensive projectile."

"That's very good strategy. I approve of your thinking," Ivan said. "And your torpedoes don't have the metal seeking capability this time, right?"

"Right, Randall can't dump shrapnel in the water to divert the torpedoes like he did in Jamaica," Eduard replied.

"You might want to go in close and try to sink them with machine guns. You have a lot of 50 caliber ammunition."

"Are you worried the torpedoes might not launch properly or Randall has defensive capability against them other then dumping a large amount of shrapnel in the water?" Eduard asked.

"I've considered the possibility."

After glancing at Yang, Ivan asked, "Have the torpedoes on these boats been tested?"

"I'm not sure about these particular boats," Yang said, "but I know they've been tested on a lot of other similar boats."

Ivan spoke back into the phone. "Ask Chung if he knows whether or not the torpedoes on the two boats have been tested."

"Hold on for a moment," Eduard said.

Ivan could hear Eduard asking the question, but he couldn't hear Chung's answer.

In a few more seconds, Ivan heard Eduard's voice again.

"Chung isn't sure, He thinks Fu Wong will know and he's calling him," Eduard said. "Give us another minute."

Ivan exhaled slowly and tapped the fingers of his right hand slowly on the table.

In just over a minute, Ivan got an answer from Eduard, but it wasn't the answer he wanted.

"Chung told me Fu doesn't know either," Eduard said. "Neither one was involved with testing the torpedoes. Chung apologized for not checking that with his contacts in Beijing. He thinks it will take too long to get that answer right now due to the time difference."

"Do the best you can," Ivan said. He disconnected.

*****

After hearing Ivan disconnect, Eduard spoke into his tactical communications unit. "We'll keep the speed at 5 knots for each of our boats and ease toward the oncoming Mark VI patrol boats. We'll get in position and then I'll give the command to fire the torpedoes, got it?"

"Got it," Taros said. "I'm looking at our pilot and he's giving me a thumbs-up to make sure I know he heard your command. We're slowing down now."

Eduard saw the pilot on his boat nod as he also gave a thumbs-up.

For the next couple of minutes, Eduard continued to study the oncoming boats.

"Stay prepared to launch the torpedoes when I give the signal," Eduard said.

"We're ready when you're ready," Chung said. "Both torpedoes are ready to launch as soon as I press the respective buttons."

Eduard also heard Fu's voice on his tactical communications unit, "Ditto over here."

*****

Colt peered out of the lead Mark VI patrol boat and focused his gaze on the stretch of water in front of him. He expected some type of trouble, but none was obvious at the moment.

Linda gestured toward the shoreline of the nearest

island. "See any kind of structure that looks like it could support launching a Poseidon Missile?"

"Not yet," Colt said. "And I'm sure it won't be obvious."

"Are you looking for anything in particular?"

"Something on the shoreline that's well camouflaged or an inlet of some kind that has some structures along the edge of the water."

"If you see an inlet like that are you taking us in close to inspect?"

"Of course," Colt said, but we'll be very cautious. They could be expecting us and waiting in ambush."

Linda pointed her device toward the shoreline and swept it left and right. "We're less than 500 yards from shore. No detection of any illegal drugs yet. No nukes either."

"Keep trying," Colt said. "Too bad we can't scan for a quantum computer or some kind of supercomputer."

"Have you received any new information about the location of the missiles?" Linda asked.

"Are you wondering if they've arrived up here?"

Linda nodded. "We should be able to detect them if they have."

Colt gave a short laugh. "Yeah, especially since the nuclear warheads are 100 megatons."

*****

Eduard stood on the deck of his stealth boat and again studied the two Mark VI patrol boats now about a half mile in front of him.

"Due to our stealth characteristics, I don't think

they've spotted us yet, but we're still about a half mile away," Eduard said into his tactical communications unit. "Hold steady and keep easing toward them. We want to get as close as we can before we fire the torpedoes. We want to maximize our chances for putting Randall and his taskforce out of action right away."

Eduard noted the pilot on his boat narrowed his eyes and seemed to concentrate on keeping their direction straight toward the middle of the two approaching boats as he kept their speed at exactly 5 knots.

"We have a good plan, but we need to be careful," Eduard spoke slowly into his communications unit. "To maximize our chances, we need to get real close before we launch the torpedoes. No loud noises."

"Yes sir," came multiple replies.

"Exactly how close do we need to get before we launch the torpedoes?" a crewman on Eduard's boat asked.

"I'm told the accuracy will be best if we're within a quarter of a mile," Eduard said. "In this case, I want to be a little bit closer. I'll give the command when I think we're close enough."

The crewman nodded slowly and didn't comment.

*****

At CIA headquarters in McLean, Paul looked at some new satellite pictures. There was something he wanted to make sure Mack was aware of. He grabbed his secure satellite phone and punched a digit.

Mack answered.

"Can you talk?" Paul asked.

"For a few seconds, but that's all. We're concentrating on inspecting the shorelines of the islands in the archipelago."

"I'm looking at the latest satellite pictures," Paul said. "Even though they have great stealth characteristics, I think I've spotted two stealth boats like the one you encountered in Jamaica. I believe it was called the Sea Ghost."

"How did you spot them?"

Paul explained and then said, "And they're about a mile from you and coming straight toward you."

"I'll alert Colt."

"Remember the maximum speed of the Mark VI is 40 miles per hour. Don't try to chase them."

"Yeah, we're all aware of our speed limitation." Mack hesitated a moment and then said, "Thanks for the information. I'll make Colt aware of this as soon as we disconnect."

"Good," Paul said. "We all need to stay closely coordinated. Charles just came rushing into my office. It looks like something real important just happened. Go ahead and talk to Colt and I'll call you back later" He disconnected.

*****

Colt heard Mack's voice come into his ear through his tactical communications unit.

"Paul just told me our latest satellite photos show two stealth boats about a mile away and coming straight toward us," Mack said.

"Two boats like the Sea Ghost we faced in Jamaica?"

"Yes," Mack said. "And they probably have torpedoes."

"If I remember correctly, they seemed to want to get close when they fired them in Jamaica."

"Do we still have shrapnel on these boats?" Mack asked.

"Yes, it's a standard defense feature."

"We'd better get ready to use it."

Colt started to comment when his secure satellite phone vibrated. He told Mack to hold on for a minute and he answered his phone.

"Have you been talking to Mack?" Grant asked.

"We're using our tactical communications units right now."

"He probably just heard from Paul, but I have some more updated information."

"What?"

"NSA intercepted a call that I think both of you will find interesting," Grant said. "The enemy stealth boats aren't using metal seeking torpedoes this time."

"So, dumping the shrapnel won't do us any good?"

"You got it."

"Any suggestions?"

"Yeah," Grant said. "Turn around and head back to base as fast as you can go."

"Why do that?" Colt asked. "You know we can't outrun them."

"Yeah, but you can buy a little time," Grant said. "I'm hoping the Navy will have time to intervene and take care of things on this one."

Colt gave the command for the boats to turn around and go full speed in the other direction.

"What will the Navy do?" Colt asked.

"They're going to use a couple of their attack helicopters. Thanks to our satellite surveillance they'll be able to home in on the stealth boats."

"How soon will they get here?"

"I'm not sure, but I've been told they left about 10 minutes ago and they're on their way from a carrier that's only 60 miles from you."

"What's the name of the carrier?"

"I was told it's a new hi-tech one. They want to keep it

secret as long as they can and they're not disclosing the name yet."

"Do you know the type of choppers?"

"They're modified versions of the SH-60B Seahawk which was primarily designed for anti-submarine warfare but can be used for a lot of other purposes, like in this case," Grant said. "I was told they can travel at 155 miles per hour so they should be getting there soon."

"Are they planning to drop bombs?"

"No, they're shooting missiles," Grant said. "I don't know what type, but I'm told they're powerful and there's going to be some big explosions."

"Any idea how big the explosions are?"

"No, but remember these helicopters are modified versions, probably well enhanced versions, of the Seahawk. They can probably carry some pretty big missiles."

Colt again looked at the stealth boats. "They'll still going slow, guess they don't know we've spotted them and think we turned around temporarily to recheck something."

"Keep going as fast as you can. Hopefully you'll be able to stay far enough away from the stealth boats to avoid being affected by the explosions."

"Once they decide we're not turning back and start chasing us they're going to overtake us quickly. I hope those choppers get here soon."

"They should be there with the next few minutes. Are the stealth boats still moving at a real slow speed?"

"Yes," Colt said. "They're just creeping along. They probably think we haven't spotted them and are waiting to see if we turn back toward them again."

"That could be true. They know they're hard to spot and they don't know we gave you the heads up about where they are," Grant replied. "I'm watching the satellite pictures and the accompanying information. They're going 5 miles an hour."

"The longer they wait to come after us the better.

Maybe we'll actually have time for the choppers to get here."

"Let's hope for that."

*****

Eduard raised his binoculars and studied the two Mark VI patrol boats. He watched them pick up speed and move in the opposite direction.

They might have spotted us, Eduard thought.

Eduard looked at the Mark VI boats again and then shrugged. It really didn't make any difference. If Randall was trying to get back to their base, they wouldn't be able to make it all the way. The stealth boats could easily catch them before they got very far along.

"It looks like Randall and his taskforce could be making a run for it," Eduard said into his tactical communications unit. "We'll wait a minute to see if they turn back toward us. If they don't we'll give chase and kick the speed up to 100 miles an hour immediately. No need to have any concern about being spotted any longer."

"Are we still going to fire the torpedoes?" Taros asked.

"We damned sure are," Eduard said. "Wait for my command. I'll still plan to fire when we're within a quarter mile of them."

Eduard spoke into his tactical communications unit, "Chung or Fu, what's the speed of our torpedoes?"

"60 miles per hour," Fu said.

"That'll work," Eduard replied. "Remember to wait for my command to fire. I might want to get a little closer under the new conditions."

"We'll wait for your signal," came two replies.

Chapter 28

Colt scanned the area behind him with his binoculars. The stealth boats were gaining fast.

Maybe I should have stopped and tried waiting a few minutes before we turned around, Colt thought as he looked at his watch. Where in the hell are the choppers?

Colt looked again at the fast-approaching stealth boats. They were now about a quarter mile behind them. He turned and looked at his pilot.

"We're absolutely going all out," the pilot of the Mark VI said. "40 miles an hour is all we can do."

Colt nodded. "Keep the petal to the metal." He noted the other Mark VI was staying alongside when he heard Mack's voice in his earpiece.

"Paul just phoned and told me he had been given authorization to contact one of the pilots of the Seahawks," Mack said. "Long story short, the pilot just told him they were only a minute away from us."

Colt looked behind him. The two stealth boats were less than a quarter mile away and it looked like they were closing the distance fast.

"Do you hear the choppers?" Mack asked with a bit of relief in his voice.

"Faintly," Colt said. "They're getting a lot louder now. They must be traveling fast."

"Damn right," Mack replied. "We've lucked out."

*****

"Do you see them?" The first helicopter pilot asked into his tactical communications unit as he reduced speed to 60 miles per hour and flew over the water about a mile in front of the two Mark VI patrol boats.

"Yep, both sets of boats," the second helicopter pilot replied, "the Mark VI's stand out, the others are difficult to see."

"Won't matter," the first pilot said. "We're fully automated and I'm getting a signal I'm locked in on the target."

"Same here."

"Let 'em fly."

*****

Eduard peered through his binoculars and watched the two oncoming helicopters that were fast approaching.

He wondered if they were there for observation.

Then he saw the two missiles launch.

A giant wave of panic hit him.

He knew it was too late now to do anything.

Colt watched the two missiles fly, one from each chopper. Almost immediately there were two giant explosions on the water behind him.

Two large plumes containing a mixture of water and smoke bellowed into the air.

Loud cheers erupted from each of the Mark VI patrol boats.

Colt felt his secure satellite phone vibrate and he answered.

"Don't worry about the cleanup," Grant said. "Several more choppers should be arriving just about now. They're different types. They'll remove the wreckage and the dead bodies. There's no chance anyone survived the type explosions the missiles produced."

Colt heard the noise and looked up.

Four big helicopters were slowing and soon hovered over the site of the explosions. Large hooks attached to the bottom of thick cables dropped toward the water. Colt noted about twenty men, probably Seals, were dressed in underwater gear and repelled down ropes to the water from the other two helicopters.

Colt spoke into his tactical communications unit, "I think we can resume our inspection of the islands."

"We're ready when you are," Mack replied.

Colt gave a signal to his pilot.

In a few minutes, both Mark VI patrol boats made a slow turn and were soon going in the opposite direction.

Colt made sure each of the boats stayed well away from the Navy activity in the area of destruction.

"Keep your speed at 15 miles per hour," Colt said into his tactical communications unit, "and get back close to shore as soon as you can."

"Roger," came several replies.

*****

In the main conference room of his headquarters in the archipelago, Ivan, Sergei, Dmitri, Pavel, and Yang continued to watch the images on the large monitor on the wall.

"Well, that was a total disaster," Ivan said. He continued to clinch his right hand into a fist, and then he started banging it on the table. He made no effort to hide his frustration as he picked up the phone with his left hand. After making an obvious effort to calm down, he punched a button.

Ivan heard Lev answer.

"Do you know what's going on?" Ivan asked.

"I was expecting your call," Lev said. "I didn't call you because I wanted to give you a chance to recover a little before we talked."

"You've been watching the satellite footage?"

"Of course I've been watching. Yuri and I have the same access to the footage as all of you do."

"Pretty bad, huh?"

"Yeah, I would say we're in a real difficult situation. This really creates a big problem for us since we've lost our Chinese computer experts. I've already made a request to Beijing to send more specialists on the new version of the Poseidon Missiles."

"Did Beijing make any more commitments?"

"Yes, but we can only get one additional person. His name is Dong Lin and he'll be here tomorrow. He speaks multiple languages in addition to Chinese, including Russian and English. I'm told he's as expert as Chung and Fu were and he'll be in frequent contact with Beijing."

"Thanks for helping," Ivan said. "And there's one other thing I'd like your help on."

"What?"

"The United States is using their Navy against us. They're obviously escalating the conflict. Maybe we should get some help from our Navy."

"Yuri has already been checking on that and some other things. He's still on the phone. We'll call and give you an answer as soon as we get one."

*****

Colt studied the scene of the explosions as the two Mark VI patrol boats went by the area at 15 miles per hour.

Getting help from the Navy had been a lifesaver. This gave him more confidence in the President.

Colt remembered the President had emphasized he wanted to avoid World War III, but he had also said he would provide more support to the taskforce if it became necessary.

No one wanted to take a chance on allowing the Poseidon Missiles to strike their targets in the United States.

Colt felt the President had really come through for them this time. He had kept his word about using more Military resources when necessary.

In a few minutes, Colt raised his binoculars and studied the area ahead. They needed to locate the site from where the two new Poseidon Missiles would be launched.

If the missiles ever got on their way, Colt figured they would be very difficult to stop.

He didn't want to have that problem. Just like they did in Jamaica, the taskforce would have to stop any missiles from being launched.

*****

In the main conference room of his headquarters, Ivan looked at Dmitri and Pavel and said, "You'll still have some help on the things Chung and Fu were going to take care of. Dong Lin will be here tomorrow and will take charge of the team of Chinese scientists."

Dmitri and Pavel both nodded.

"Some of the scientists don't speak Russian or English. They only speak Chinese," Ivan said. "Dong speaks all three languages and he'll be here tomorrow. I don't think we'll have to worry about everyone being able to communicate now."

"How soon will the two Poseidon missiles get here?" Dmitri asked.

"I still don't know," Ivan said. "It should be soon. If we haven't heard anything by the time Dong gets here, I'll have him check with Beijing on that as soon as he arrives."

"Are we getting any more Russian assassins?" Pavel asked. "We just lost some more good ones."

"Lev and Yuri know that," Ivan said. "I didn't ask, but I know they'll treat it as a priority."

Ivan started to say more and then reached for his ringing phone. He could see it was Lev calling and he answered.

"We have it worked out where you're getting another expect Russian assassin," Lev said. "His name is Taras Popov and he'll be there tomorrow. He and Dong should both arrive during the morning."

"Do you have any news about whether our Navy will help or not?"

"We're still working on that. We'll keep you posted."

Ivan heard Lev disconnect and then he gave the latest

news to the group sitting around him.

*****

In the J. Edgar Hoover Building in Washington DC, Ken, Frank, and Steve sat around the large table in the main conference room.

"Do we have any good information yet on the location of the launch site?" Ken asked.

"Not completely," Steve said. "NRO has identified 6 potential locations, and their analysts are doing a lot of research. But they haven't come up with anything conclusive yet."

Frank narrowed his eyes and looked at Steve. "Any guesses if they will?"

"Come up with anything conclusive?" Steve asked.

Frank grunted. "I think that's the subject."

Steve shrugged. "I haven't talked to any of the analysts today. I don't want to interrupt them."

"Give me your best guess," Frank said.

"Yes," Steve said. "I think they're get it figured out but I don't know how quickly they'll be able to do it."

Frank gave a slow nod and didn't comment.

"We know Ivan Titov is a smart guy and I'm guessing he's still following an overall strategy developed by the chess masters in the Kremlin," Ken said. "As we did before, we need to concentrate on making smarter moves than he does. And this time we need to put him and Sergei out of business for good."

Frank grunted and turned toward Steve. "You've been keeping up with all the technical details. Are we looking at current satellite footage?" He gestured toward the numerous large monitors positioned in various locations around the four walls.

"Yes," Steve said. "It's all live. We're tied directly into the NRO surveillance system for that area."

Frank clinched a fist. "This time we need to give all these bastards what they deserve, specifically Ivan and Sergei."

"NRO and NSA have made this mission their top priority," Ken said. "And just before this meeting, I was informed NSA was in the process of decrypting some new phone call intercepts. For us to make smarter moves than Ivan Titov and Sergei Nikitin all agencies need to coordinate even closer and we're all trying to do that."

"Should you give Charles a call and see if he has any updates that we don't have?" Frank asked.

"I talked to him just before this meeting," Ken said. "He's the one who informed me about NSA. He's currently discussing things with his staff in McLean." Ken looked at his watch. "We're going to compare notes again in thirty minutes."

"Steve and I will call Grant in a few minutes and discuss his latest thinking on all this," Frank said. "He's still talking directly with Colt and he's keeping Harlan Pierce and Jim Boxer at Boswic fully informed. I think we're all doing a good job of staying right on top of this thing. We're investigating every aspect of the developments as they happen."

Steve pointed toward one of the monitors. "I think Colt and the taskforce might have sighted something. It looks like both Mark VI patrol boats are pulling into a small harbor."

"I hope they've found a launch site," Ken said, "This thing could sure as hell get out of hand in a hurry if Ivan Titov and Sergei Nikitin outsmart us and are able to launch the Poseidon Missiles."

*****

At CIA headquarters in McLean, Director Charles Andrews looked across the large solid oak table in the main conference room at Paul Collins and Nick Wallace.

Various live satellite images of Colt and the taskforce were on all the large monitors lining the walls.

"Ken told me he's hoping we can find the missile launch site real soon," Charles said. "It looks like Colt and Mack might have found something that's requires some investigation." He pointed toward one of the monitors.

Nick pointed to another one of the monitors. "I'm guessing they found something of real interest."

Paul laughed and punched Nick on the shoulder. "A brilliant deduction, amazing you could figure that out."

Charles laughed too.

There was a brief silence.

"Okay," Charles said. "It's good we're not too uptight. Let's hope we make some good progress real soon."

Chapter 29

A few hours later, Ivan, Sergei, Dmitri, Pavel, and Yang remained in the main conference room of the headquarters building in the archipelago and continued to watch the images on various large monitors on the walls.

Ivan reached for his ringing phone. Again, he could see it was Lev calling. He answered.

"The missiles will be arriving in less than an hour," Lev said with a high level of optimism in his voice.

Ivan glanced at the wall monitors and then asked, "How do you know? I don't see anything on the satellite images."

"Yuri and I just got a call from Beijing. Their top missile scientist just told me the missiles are 25 miles south of you, traveling north at a depth of 30 feet and going 50 miles per hour."

"We'll get ready to receive them," Ivan said. "We'll get the mobile launchers down to the water and get ready to load them."

"How are you going to do that?"

"About a quarter mile south of our headquarters building, we have a large 10-foot-thick concrete slab that runs down to the water. We have a good method to lift the missiles out of the water and move them to our hi-tech armament building we'll use to prepare them for launch."

"Are you currently setup to do all that?"

"We've been prepared for over a week. The Chinese scientists have fine-tuned all the equipment," Ivan said. "We have special launch vehicles designed to pick them up and move them to the armament building. When we're ready, we'll use those same vehicles to take them back to the water for launching."

"Good luck."

"Don't worry. We're well prepared for this."

"The Americans will see everything you're doing, and they'll know where you take them."

"I don't think so."

"How're you going to prevent that?"

Ivan explained.

*****

At CIA headquarters in McLean, Director Charles Andrews looked across the large solid oak table in the main conference room at Paul Collins and Nick Wallace.

Various live satellite images of Colt and the taskforce were on some of the large monitors lining the walls. Other live satellite images were on the remaining monitors.

"I think the taskforce has definitely found the area for the missile launch site," Charles said. He pointed toward one of the monitors that showed the taskforce about a mile away from where two large vehicles were traveling north from the water's edge on one of the islands. "I'm sure those vehicles are each carrying a large missile. Having solid tops isn't going to fool us."

Paul nodded. "I'm sure you're right and it's on the same island we think Ivan Titov is using for his headquarters."

"I've been studying that island for a long time. They built a large concrete slab a few weeks ago that runs down to the water and then they covered it, along with a large area around it, with a high roof of camouflage netting." Nick looked at Charles and Paul. "Unfortunately, we can't follow the missiles all the way to where they're taking them. They'll quickly get into a lot of thick forest."

"Yeah," Paul said. "We know from intercepted phone calls that island is one of the islands Titov developed for his military purposes. And we suspect that's where he has his headquarters, but we've never been able to get a clear satellite image due to all his camouflage techniques and the thick forest."

Charles grunted. "We'll need to have Colt and the taskforce check it out as soon as they can get there." He picked up his phone and punched a button. "I'll make sure everyone else is following this latest development."

After Charles finished his call, he glanced at Paul and Nick. "Ken will make sure everyone else is in sync with us. That includes alerting Grant to give Colt a call and bring him up to date."

"This mission is definitely more over the top than the one in Jamaica," Paul said. "It has almost limitless complications and Ivan Titov is on his home turf this time."

There was a brief silence.

"If these new versions of the Poseidon Missile get launched, we have some huge problems to resolve immediately," Charles said. "Colt's main job as leader of the taskforce is to make damned sure they don't get launched."

Paul gave a slight nod as he glanced at his watch. "Colt should be getting the latest update from Grant within the next few minutes. Hopefully he'll make some real progress quickly."

"This time Colt needs to make sure he and the taskforce put Ivan and Sergei out of business for good," Charles said.

Paul looked at Nick. "Are you still keeping up with all the technical details and are we looking at current satellite footage?" He gestured toward the numerous large monitors positioned in various locations around the four walls."

"Yes to both questions," Nick said. He looked at some laptop computers on the table in front of him "All the images are live. We're still tied directly into the NRO surveillance system for that area."

Charles reached for his phone. "I'll give Ken another call and discuss the details of his latest conversation with Grant. We all damned sure better stay in close sync if we want to succeed."

Chapter 30

At Boswic in Tampa, Harlan stared across his desk at Jim. "I got the latest information from Grant, and I hope Colt can handle everything. It looks like he found one of Titov's outposts and he's moving in the direction of the launch site. I'm sure it's heavily guarded."

"Colt has proven many times he can rise to the occasion when he needs to handle difficult tasks."

"This mission has more complications than the one in Jamaica and Ivan Titov is on his home turf." After gesturing to Jim, Harlan stood and walked back to the round mahogany conference table in a corner of his spacious office.

Harlan exhaled sharply and plopped down in a well-padded chair.

Jim followed and eased into a chair across from Harlan.

"Colt being in charge puts all the pressure on Boswic

to produce the desired results which is a complete victory for the United States," Harlan said, "and this mission has thousands of complications. If those huge new versions of the Poseidon Missile get launched and if the United States somehow survives and continues to function, we're never going to get another project with the CIA or the FBI."

"We're paid big bucks for Colt leading the taskforce and I'm confident Colt and Linda will handle things real well. They also have a great team of agents. Mack is one of the best fighters on the planet."

"So, you're not real concerned?" Harlan asked.

"About Colt performing well?"

"That's the subject we're on," Harlan said gruffly. He stared at Jim. "Remember Colt never had to endure all the rigorous tasks we had to handle in the Marines. He might have a lot of talent, but he's never had to handle what we did."

Jim flashed a look of irritation. "Some people think he had to handle even tougher tasks. Delta Force has a stellar reputation."

Harlan grunted and didn't comment.

"Just giving you some feedback," Jim said. "Ken Johnson and Charles Andrews both think Colt went through the best training available. Remember Colt also went through a couple of their most advanced training programs before they selected him as the taskforce leader on the previous missions."

"We should have pulled some strings and gotten him scheduled for advanced Marine training."

"Two years ago, he went through the Robin Sage exercise given by the Special Warfare Training Group. Don't forget they told us Colt was the best who had ever gone through there."

Harlan rolled his eyes. "Nothing is as tough as Marine training."

"You should be over your concern by now about Colt

being cocky. Colt has performed well on all his previous missions and I'm sure he'll keep it up."

"He's still too cocky. You should admit that."

Jim hesitated for a couple of seconds and then shrugged. "Maybe he's still a little cocky, but that doesn't seem to cause any problems with anyone. That could be to his advantage."

"Well, it continues to bug the hell out of me." Harlan flicked his right hand. "Just wait, his cockiness is going to lead to a big screw-up eventually. That will reflect badly on us and cause a problem in getting future business."

Jim leaned forward. "Are you telling me Ken and Charles can't judge character?"

"Ken and Charles don't work directly with Colt," Harlan said sharply, "and we do."

"They see him often enough and they know a lot about him."

"I don't argue that," Harlan said. "But I still think they could be missing something."

Jim gestured with both palms out. "Colt leading the taskforce is a great endorsement for Boswic and Linda also being a member of the taskforce is another great endorsement for us."

Harlan stood, walked over to a pot of freshly brewed coffee, and filled a couple of ceramic mugs. He carried them back to the table and placed one in front of Jim. "I'll continue to give this some more thought. Maybe I'll end up with a different opinion."

"If it makes you feel any better, I'll keep reminding Colt to keep his ego under control," Jim said. "Don't forget I've lectured him a few times in the past about that."

Harlan gave a slight nod as he glanced at his watch. "We should be getting another update from Grant within the next few minutes. Hopefully, Colt is about to make some real progress."

*****

In the main conference room in his headquarters, Ivan scanned the faces around the large table. Sergei, Dmitri, Pavel, and Yang sat around him.

"We want to stay at least one move ahead of Randall and his taskforce," Ivan said.

Dmitri gave a short laugh. "You're still referring to the chess strategy?"

"I don't care what kind of strategy it is as long as it works," Ivan said. "I just follow the strategy Lev and Yuri send to us."

Dmitri pointed toward one of the monitors on the wall. "It looks like the taskforce has docked their boats in the harbor just south of us. Are you ready for them?"

Pavel looked at Ivan. "And, if you are ready for them, what are you planning to do?

"Of course I'm ready." Ivan glanced at Sergei. "Tell us what preparations you've made."

"We've planned for this very thing. We have a large number of assassins close to the waterfront waiting for them to come in this direction," Sergei said. "And if they do come this way as we expect, they won't get very far before they come under heavy fire."

Yang looked quizzically at Sergei. "How good are the assassins you have defending this area?"

"They don't have all the talents you and Taras have, but there are a lot of them," Sergei said. "I think they'll provide an excellent defense. We'll put you and Taras into the fight if we need you. There are only 20 of them coming after us and we should be able to eliminate every last one of the bastards before they get close to our headquarters building."

Pavel narrowed his eyes. "They're moving toward our launch site. That could pose a problem for launching the missiles quickly."

"We have the missiles in a safe area, but we won't have them ready to launch before tomorrow afternoon at the earliest," Sergei said. "We should have Randall and his taskforce out of our way by then, Mark VI patrol boats and their pilots included."

Yang leaned forward. "I want to have the first chance to eliminate Randall."

"We'll see how things work out. I don't care who eliminates him as long as someone does," Ivan said. He gave Yang a long stare.

Yang returned Ivan's stare but made no comment.

*****

Following the latest recommendations he had received from Grant, Colt led the taskforce along the waterfront and moved toward the east.

Grant had assured him that everyone stateside was coordinated.

"Our experts think we're going directly toward what will be the launch area for the missiles," Colt said into his tactical communications microphone. "They'll probably use mobile launchers on wheels to get the missiles to the water."

"They must be damned big launchers to hold missiles that are 80 feet long and 8 feet wide," Mack replied.

"Right," Colt said. "And I'm sure they've been made especially for this situation. We'll continue east into the woods and look around. Our satellites are zeroed in on the general area, but there are too many woods to distinguish any structures. We'll have to scout around a bit."

"Do you know if Grant is making the strategic decisions for the taskforce?" Linda asked.

"I don't know but he's clearly the one discussing our tactics with us right now," Colt said.

"Paul told me the CIA and FBI agreed it was best to keep Grant fully up to date on all the available information and let him pass it along to us," Mack replied. "Grant will convey the strategic decisions we should follow, and everyone still wants you to make the tactical decisions when we encounter any resistance."

Colt grinned. "Guess we're as organized as we can be for the moment. Let's hope we can execute as well as we need to when the time comes."

Mack and Linda returned the grin.

Colt was glad they could stay loose and not get too uptight. In his opinion, that was a key characteristic of true professionals.

Chapter 31

Grant tried to relax as much as he could, but he had a lot on his mind. He figured some brilliant thinking from the Kremlin was still driving the Russian strategy.

The Kremlin continued to stay in the background, but Grant knew they were spearheading another initiative to bring down the United States with China's help. He knew both Russia and China wanted to gain dominance in the world. If they did bring down the United States, who would end up in charge? Grant shrugged and turned his thinking back to the immediate situation.

It was certain Russia would try again to launch more of their Poseidon Missiles and China was still involved.

Grant started to think about the best recommendations to give Colt just as a call came through on his secure line. He glanced at the caller ID and answered.

"Got new information," Ken said, "just finished discussing it with Frank and Steve." He relayed the information and then asked, "Are you still keeping in close contact with Harlan?"

"Yes, I'll make sure he has all the new data."

"I've already sent him a full report. He has all the information I just gave you. He should be able to discuss it when you call."

"So, we're certain both Russian and Chinese surveillance satellites are tracking our taskforce, and Ivan Titov knows their exact position on his island?"

"I'm sure he at least knows they're somewhere in the woods around him."

"Colt has known for a long time he's being closely watched. And he knows he can ask for help as soon as he thinks he needs some," Grant said. "And he's continuing to be careful to not fall into some traps. Again, I'll urge Colt to not take any extreme risks."

Ken gave a short laugh. "And again, do you think you and Colt have the same definition of extreme risks?"

Grant also gave a short laugh. "I'll just make sure he knows we'll provide more help anytime he makes the request."

"Go ahead and call him and discuss the latest details. I'll keep you posted on any new developments."

"Sounds like a plan."

After Ken disconnected, Grant punched a digit on his phone and heard Colt answer.

"Are things okay?" Grant asked.

"We're still moving east through thick woods and we haven't run into any opposition yet," Colt said.

"We have lot of new information," Grant replied. "Due to some of our newest technology, we now know there are four large structures in the woods around you. You and your taskforce need to check them out. You're close to some of them. I'll try to give you more details as soon as I get them."

"Do we continue to move east?"

"Yes," Grant said. "The first one you need to check is about a half mile from you. All the others are further inland. We'll keep you informed as well as we can."

"Any clues as to what's in the structures?"

"We think the missiles are in one of them and are being prepared for launch. There are probably a lot of drugs in the others. That's still one of their booming businesses to make a lot of money and finance their activities."

"Why do you think some of the structures are warehouses for drugs?"

"NSA has intercepted a lot of calls, and they've been able to decrypt a lot of content from many of the conversations," Grant said. "Okay, here are the latest details pertaining to your situation up there." He took a few minutes to explain.

After getting the update from Grant, Colt led his team of twenty toward the first structure.

Knowing they would be under surveillance by multiple satellites anytime they entered an open area, Colt made sure they kept the best possible cover they could as they proceeded. That wasn't difficult due to the thick woods.

Chapter 32

Colt and the taskforce all clad in camouflage fatigues continued through the thick woods until they came within about twenty yards of a large structure with huge tree limbs overhanging the roof.

No wonder our satellites couldn't detect any buildings in these woods, Colt thought.

Along with the nineteen other taskforce members, Colt hid in thick foliage south of the large structure. They took several minutes to carefully study the situation.

There was no obvious activity.

Colt was again the overall leader of the two teams of ten each. He and Linda were on Team One. Mack led Team Two.

"Weapons check," Colt whispered into his tactical microphone. "Make sure you're ready for action."

Colt checked his silenced SIG 556 rifle that could fire 900 rounds per minute and ensured it was loaded with a full magazine. He also checked the four spare magazines. They each had 30 5.56 mm NATO cartridges. He then checked the Glock 19 pistol he carried in a tactical holster on his right thigh. The magazine had 15 high powered full metal jacket rounds. He carried four spare magazines for his Glock.

Some agents had chosen different weapons.

For a rifle, some had chosen a Heckler & Koch MP5/10 A2 with an integral suppressor (a silencer). These models also used a 30-round magazine, but they fired 10mm bullets at 800 rounds per minute in full automatic mode.

Colt knew the A2 variant had a fixed stock and weighed only 5.6 pounds, unloaded. He also knew most MP5's fired 9mm ammunition, but these custom models delivered a bit more power using 10mm rounds.

For pistols, some carried the Smith & Wesson .357 Magnum revolver in a tactical holster on the thigh. In case the enemy had protective clothing, they wanted better penetrating capability. Others carried a Sig-Sauer P226 for their pistol. He still preferred his SIG 556 rifle and his Glock 19 pistol.

He had everyone set their rifles on semi-automatic or single-shot firing mode. Since it looked like most of the upcoming action would likely occur inside the building, the danger of ricochets made use of a multi-shot firing mode inadvisable.

Each member of the taskforce also had two smoke grenades and two concussion grenades.

In addition to grenades and the other weapons, every taskforce member had tactical communications gear, night-vision goggles, protective masks against various chemical attacks, and helmet-mounted infrared flashlights. If the lighting was insufficient inside the building they were getting ready to enter, he knew they still could navigate in dark areas.

He knew they were well equipped to storm the place,

and he waved everyone forward toward the building which was well camouflaged with multiple shades of brown on the concrete walls.

They used maximum stealth and quickly surrounded the building. Everyone stayed behind heavy growth a few yards from the outside walls.

After Mack used his toolkit to open the back door, the 20 members of the taskforce used extreme caution and made their entry two at a time.

Colt and Linda entered last and huddled behind a row of stacked wooden crates about 10 yards from the door. He whispered into his tactical microphone and issued instructions.

Knowing overconfidence was a potential weakness, he scanned the area with great caution as his team spread out across the hundred-yard-width of the giant structure and moved forward.

Everyone kept their tactical microphones activated and stayed in constant contact.

There, to his left, in the shadows. Colt spotted movement out of the corner of one eye, but too late. A figure reached around the corner of a stack of crates and grabbed the barrel of his SIG 556.

The figure jerked hard.

Colt released the rifle and stepped back, staying evenly balanced. He saw a knife flash in the dim light.

Taking another step back, Colt moved his Glock 19 from the holster with a fluid sliding motion. He executed a quick forward snap, aimed at his target, and pulled the trigger.

A muffled pop sounded.

The figure with the knife went down instantly. The knife clanged on the concrete floor. The smell of gunpowder hung in the air. The whole thing happened within a couple of seconds.

Colt dropped to a semi-crouch and kept his balance on

both feet while scanning for more combatants. After seeing no more threats, he holstered his Glock and retrieved his SIG 556.

"One assassin eliminated," Colt said into his tactical microphone. He gave a quick explanation.

After completing a thorough search, the taskforce found no other threats in the first warehouse. They found a lot of drugs though. They opened some of the crates and found they all contained a special blend of marijuana.

Since all the crates they had opened were well separated throughout the structure, everyone concluded they had entered one of the drug warehouses Ivan Titov maintained to support his drug trafficking operations.

Colt left two men behind to secure the place and then moved outside and led his remaining team of 18 northward. He spoke into his tactical microphone, "Single file and keep five yards apart."

The taskforce moved smoothly through the thick woods. A few birds made a variety of chirping noises in the treetops, seeming unperturbed by the stealthy force flowing beneath them.

After a few minutes of gliding under thick overhanging branches, Colt signaled a halt and gestured to Linda and Mack. They eased up to his position.

"Someone at a guard post," Colt whispered. He pointed. "We need to eliminate him without making any noise."

Linda and Mack nodded.

"You go get him," Mack said. "You have the highest marks in all of our training on hand-to-hand combat."

Preparing for action, Colt felt an emotion of satisfaction mixed with extreme caution.

He saw the guard wasn't looking in his direction and he moved forward as quickly and as silently as he could.

The guard started to turn in Colt's direction.

Colt increased his speed. When he realized he wasn't

going to get to the guard in time, he knew he couldn't let a gunshot alert the opposing force. He aimed and fired. The guard fell; the only sound, a muffled pop. Colt continued forward.

As he closed on the guard post, he saw another man appear.

The man was backing toward him and looking the other way—toward the north.

Colt figured there was another structure probably just a little north of their position. He didn't want to shoot the guard in the back, but he didn't want to take any big chances either. Colt intentionally stepped on a branch.

Instantly moving his AK-47 to firing position, the guard turned quickly in Colt's direction.

Colt fired. The only sound was a muffled pop.

The guard immediately dropped his rifle and fell to the ground.

Colt waved everyone forward.

They soon arrived at another large structure that looked exactly the same as the first.

"I'll give Grant a status update and then we'll search inside," Colt said into his tactical microphone. "It's probably another warehouse." He grabbed his secure satellite phone from a pocket.

Before he made his call, his phone vibrated. He checked the Caller ID and answered.

"I have some interesting new information. Are you safe at the moment?" Grant asked.

"Yes," Colt said. "Everything is stable for us right now and we're in good cover."

"Okay, give me your status."

He gave his status report and listened for a few moments. He then disconnected and spoke into his tactical microphone, "Grant thinks his team of analysts might have discovered the exact location of the structure the Poseidon Missiles are in. One of our satellites has some type of equipment for long range detection of nuclear material. They need to do some more analysis before they're sure. Grant will get back to me as soon as they finish."

"So where does that leave us?" Mack asked.

"We'll start inspecting this next warehouse and be prepared to break off real soon. If Grant calls and tells us the analysts are correct, we'll go straight toward the location of the missiles," Colt said. "It's critical we don't allow any of them to be launched."

"So, we're going to continue with this warehouse or whatever this structure is for right now?" Linda asked.

"Right," Colt said. "But be ready to disengage quickly if Grant calls and confirms the location of the missiles."

Chapter 33

At CIA headquarters in McLean, six people gathered in a hi-tech conference room with a line of large monitors on each wall. Different images were on each monitor.

Charles Andrews, CIA Director, Paul Collins, head of the Terrorist Threat Investigation Unit, and Nick Wallace, Technology Specialist were there from the CIA.

Ken Johnson, FBI Director, Frank Hellman, head of the Special Investigation Unit for Domestic Threats, and Steve Lockett, Technology Specialist represented the FBI.

"The taskforce is cutting off a lot of funding from the illegal drug business to Titov and his henchmen and probably doing a lot of damage to the status of the Russian Chinese partnership," Ken said.

Charles nodded. "And as soon as we get the necessary details we'll send the taskforce to where the missiles are located."

"Yeah, and we have to be careful to avoid a trap," Ken said. "We know the Russian strategy for world domination is some weird combination of poker and chess tactics and they're still playing for high stakes."

"It still looks like the chess masters are developing the

initial strategy, but the people executing, namely Ivan Titov, are employing the characteristics of professional poker players. They obviously have some flexibility," Charles replied. "But we have to be sure we have the correct data before we send more details to Grant." He gestured to Paul.

"I'm guessing Titov is going to use more cyber warfare as this thing goes forward," Paul said. "We know they still have a quantum computer, and we know they still have some supercomputers."

Steve leaned forward. "We've determined the villains have at least four supercomputer sites: one in Moscow, two in Beijing, and one in the archipelago off the west coast of Finland. Various hacking attempts are still coming from all four of these locations."

"Do you still think the supercomputer in the archipelago is in Titov's headquarters?" Frank asked.

"Yes," Charles said. "And we think the quantum computer is there too."

"Ivan Titov and Sergei Nikitin have a direct connection to every threat we're concerned about." Ken scanned the faces around the table. "They definitely need to be eliminated this time. We can't let them loose again."

"Has NSA or the NRO been able to determine the exact coordinates of his headquarters location in the archipelago yet?" Ken asked.

"No," Paul said, "but I know they're all constantly working hard to do that. It's likely his headquarters and the missiles are in the same general location."

*****

In the Kremlin, Lev sat at the large mahogany desk in his office and looked at Yuri who was sitting in front of him.

"Randall and his taskforce are causing us a lot of problems again," Lev said. "They have to be eliminated as soon as possible."

"Do you know how close to the missiles they are?"

"Real close." Lev grunted. "It's a good thing we separated them and built two different structures to prepare them for launch."

"So exactly how close is Randall and his taskforce?"

Lev's eyes flashed. "They're less than two miles from the first structure."

"And the second structure is another two miles from the first one, right?"

Lev nodded slowly.

"Can't we ask for some air support from our superiors?"

"Do you have jets or helicopters in mind?"

"I think we should be able to use some attack helicopters like our enemy did, don't you?"

"We should be able to respond in kind to what the United States did. That shouldn't spark another world war."

Yuri nodded and said, "Are you going to make that request right now?"

"I will in a few minutes."

Yuri leaned forward. "We don't have much time."

"I know, but we need to wait for Randall and his group to get close to a sparser area before we request the helicopters. The helicopters can't attack them very well in the thick forest."

"Do you know if Ivan has security installed in the drug warehouse Randall is close to?"

"I'll call him and check. And I'll call our superiors and request the helicopters. If they agree with doing that, the helicopter crews will probably need a little time to prepare. Even if Ivan's security can't stop Randall's taskforce, they should be able to buy the helicopter crews some time."

"It's likely Ivan has the security installed, but we also

need to make sure Ivan will get a signal if someone breaks into the warehouse."

Lev nodded as he picked up the phone.

*****

In the main conference room in his headquarters in the archipelago, Ivan answered his ringing phone as he scanned the faces around the large table.

Sergei, Taras, and Yang were the only ones there.

Dmitri, Pavel, and Dong had moved to the structures being used to prepare the missiles for launch. They had left to further assist the scientists who were doing the bulk of the work.

"Do you know the exact location of Randall and his taskforce right now?" Lev asked.

"No," Ivan said. "We can't track them in the thick forest."

"Isn't another one of your drug warehouses the next structure in the path we think they're taking?"

"Yes."

"Do you have it wired with your best security equipment?"

"Of course, and we should get a signal if they break in."

"Did you get a signal when they broke into the first drug warehouse?"

"No, we only knew they were there because they eliminated our guards."

"How could they disable your automated security without you knowing about it?"

"We don't know, but somehow they did."

"Damn."

There was a brief silence.

“Give me the exact coordinates of the locations where the two missiles are being prepared for launch.”

“Are you going to request some air support?”

“Yes,” Lev said impatiently. “Yuri and I are going to request some attack helicopters. Now give me the coordinates.

With an element of relief in his voice, Ivan gave the coordinates and he heard Lev disconnect.

Ivan looked at Sergei, Taras, and Yang as he explained what Lev had told him.

“So, Lev doesn’t know yet if his superiors will approve the helicopters?” Taras asked.

“No,” Ivan said, “but at least he’s going to ask.”

“Why wouldn’t they approve?” Yang asked. “We would only be responding in kind to what the Americans have already done.”

Ivan set his jaw as his gaze rested directly on Yang. “You have a good point and I hope you’re right.’

“What do you expect?” Taras asked, looking at Ivan.

Ivan shrugged. “It’s always hard to tell what the Kremlin will do.”

Sergei leaned forward, tightened his lips, and then said, “Let’s hope the leaders at the Kremlin make the right decision. We might need some help getting rid of Randall and the taskforce.”

*****

In McLean, Charles picked up his vibrating phone and answered.

“When will that happen?” he asked after listening for a moment.

He listened for a few moments more and then thanked them for calling and disconnected.

Charles scanned the faces around him. “NSA just decrypted some more information from an intercepted call, and they discovered Ivan Titov might be getting some helicopter support from the Kremlin.”

“How soon will the helicopters show up?” Paul asked.

“The spokesperson at NSA told me they haven’t found that out yet,” Charles said. “They’re hoping to get some more details when they intercept more calls.”

“We need to make Grant aware of the helicopter threat so he can alert Colt.” Ken picked up his phone and pushed a button.

After Ken finished his call, Frank asked, “Has any additional information been uncovered about the exact coordinates of Titov’s headquarters on the island?”

“NSA is still decrypting information from several intercepted calls, and we have over a hundred analysts here at the CIA working on the tons of information we already have,” Charles said. He glanced at Ken. “I’m sure you have a lot of analyst going through all the same information at the FBI.”

Ken nodded and made no comment.

There was a brief silence.

“We have to make sure the Poseidon Missiles are never launched.” Paul clinched a fist. “We need to locate them and then wait for Colt and his team to deactivate them. Even if we get the coordinates of exactly where they’re located, we can’t take a chance on exploding 100 megaton nuclear warheads with a bombing raid or a missile strike. We’ll have to wait on Colt and the taskforce to do their thing.”

“We need to get those coordinates soon,” Ken said.

Paul nodded and gave a thumbs-up. “We certainly can’t let the Russians and Chinese launch any of the Poseidon Missiles.”

“Maybe NSA and NRO can come up with the necessary information before it’s too late,” Steve said.

"Hopefully they will," Nick replied. "Also, the taskforce might find some information in one of the warehouses that would help, especially if they find a warehouse housing the supercomputer or a quantum computer."

Steve nodded. "Or both."

Nick gave a thumbs-up.

More discussion followed that lasted for about thirty minutes.

Chapter 34

Colt disconnected from his phone call and spoke into his tactical communications unit, "The enemy might be sending some attack helicopters to intercept us. Stay on the alert."

"Roger," came multiple replies.

"Do you know how soon that might happen?" Mack asked.

"Grant told me NSA thinks that's still being worked out by the Kremlin," Colt said. "Based on all the analysis he received, he doesn't expect it will be happening real soon."

"So, we're going to continue our current plan on what we're doing?" Mack asked.

"Right," Colt said. "Let's go check this building. If it's another warehouse, it might not be that well defended inside."

Colt led his remaining team of 18 warriors toward the back entrance of the structure. They moved in single file and remained five yards apart.

After Mack used his tools to open a back door, they verified it was indeed another warehouse.

The taskforce split into groups of two and spread out across the width of the floor, which looked to be about sixty yards.

A group of two moved up each of the nine aisles toward the front. The concrete floor in the huge warehouse appeared to be about one hundred yards long.

The now familiar musty smell from stored drugs hung in the air.

"Someone's ahead, twenty yards," Colt said. He glanced at Linda. "I'm going to capture this guy. You want to come along?"

"Roger. I'll stay close behind you."

After easing through the shadows to within about thirty feet of his target, Colt stepped into the open with his SIG 556 pointed at the man's head.

"Freeze and drop the weapon," Colt said.

Linda also pointed her rifle at the assassin.

The assassin released his grip on the AK-47. It bounced on the floor. He didn't move.

"We might need to take him out before he causes us any trouble," Linda said.

"Stay ready to do that."

Linda nodded and kept her rifle pointed at the man's chest.

Colt had an uneasy feeling.

The assassin didn't seem to have any fear, Colt thought. He figured the heavily muscled man would probably fight to the death.

Linda moved closer to the assassin.

"Be careful," Colt said.

The assassin turned fully toward Linda as she

approached.

Colt quickly realized he had spoken too late.

With amazing speed, the assassin kicked the rifle out of Linda's hand and dropped her to the floor with a chop to the neck.

As Colt rushed forward, the assassin spun toward him.

Feeling a wave of urgency to check on Linda, who was lying motionless on the floor, Colt squeezed off a quick shot.

The bullet struck something solid, but the combatant didn't fall.

Bulletproof vest, Colt thought as he continued forward.

Colt closed in while keeping his weapon trained on his adversary's head.

A prisoner to interrogate could be a useful way to get more information about the setup around here. He didn't really want to kill the guy unless he had to.

Colt took a quick glance at Linda. She was moaning and thrashing around a little.

Was she going to be okay? Did she need some immediate attention?

Feeling a flash of urgency, Colt moved closer to the assassin.

The muscular assassin stood motionless, smirking.

As he continued toward the assassin, Colt, uncharacteristically, got a little impatient. He felt the need to check on Linda. She might be recovering, but she might need some immediate help.

Colt made his move too hastily, big mistake on his part.

The assassin perfectly executed a front snap-kick at Colt's rifle and the SIG 556 clanged on the concrete floor.

Now the two men faced each other without weapons.

Colt regretted the strap over his Glock 19 was still in place as he stared at the muscular assassin. He saw no fear, only supreme confidence.

"Who are you?" Colt asked crisply.

The assassin grinned. "No one you know, Randall."

Still feeling a strong sense of urgency, Colt reacted. His straight punch toward the chin of the assassin was blocked. He tried more punches and several kicks that also met blocks.

This muscular man in front of him was an excellent fighter, Colt thought. He knew he must rise to the occasion quickly. He needed to check on Linda as soon as possible.

This was indeed a challenge.

Exhaling sharply, Colt threw more punches.

They all met blocks.

Colt struggled to find an opening. An inkling of frustration crept into his thoughts.

The thought that he needed to defeat this Russian bastard quickly and check on Linda dominated his actions.

The assassin took a step back. Colt glanced in Linda's direction. To his immense relief, he noticed she had gotten to her feet, good.

While the assassin continued to look at Colt, Linda quickly moved toward the muscular assassin. She didn't slow down to scoop up her SIG 556.

Apparently feeling his own need for urgency, the assassin rushed forward, away from Linda, and executed a flying kick toward Colt's chest.

Colt blocked the kick but was knocked backwards a few feet.

The enemy combatant immediately spun away from Colt and toward Linda.

Linda landed a hard punch just under the assassin's lower right rib cage. Colt saw that the punch had no effect.

"He's wearing a bullet-proof vest," Colt said, as he assessed the best move to make without conflicting with what Linda was doing.

"You bastard, you caught me by surprise before, but you won't do it again." Linda unleashed a vicious kick toward the assassin's groin.

The kick was blocked.

Linda took a few steps back.

Colt charged the assassin, who was now five yards away.

The assassin dove away from Colt and Linda and reached for his AK-47 on the floor near him.

Within a couple of seconds, Colt released the strap over his Glock 19 and drew.

The assassin swung the AK-47 toward Colt.

Colt fired three quick rounds at the assassin's head.

The enemy combatant collapsed into a mangled heap. He obviously had died instantly.

Colt looked at Linda. "You okay?"

"Yeah, I'm okay," Linda said. "The bastard landed a lucky punch earlier. I should have been more careful."

Colt grinned.

Linda returned the grin as she dusted herself off.

"Glad you eliminated him." Linda said, looking directly at Colt.

Colt nodded.

"That bastard was really good," Linda said slowly. "I've never lost a fight before."

Colt shrugged. "Lucky I didn't lose, otherwise we'd both be dead."

Linda stared at Colt for a moment and then said, "I noticed you weren't doing so well yourself when I got to my feet. So don't rub it in."

"Just a thought that came to mind," Colt said, as he grabbed his comm unit off the floor and blew off the dust.

When he ensured it was still working, he gave a quick report to his team. So far, no one else had encountered any enemy combatants.

He and Linda continued moving toward the front of the warehouse. The floor in front of them was empty. He glanced at Linda. She appeared to be in good form. The swelling around her temple was minimal.

"You sure you're okay?" Colt asked.

"In the Marines, I got worse knocks than this in my training," Linda said, her eyes narrowing a little. "They didn't go easy on the women." She gave a slight grin. "Everyone got equal treatment."

He also gave a slight grin. He was glad he and Linda had similar attitudes. It was never good to get uptight.

"Keep moving up the aisles toward the front of the warehouse," Colt spoke into his tactical microphone. "We need to ensure any assassins in this place have been eliminated before we secure it and move on."

When they reached the front of the warehouse and had encountered no more assassins, Colt again left two men to secure the warehouse and, using extreme caution, led the remaining 16 members of the taskforce out the front entrance and into the woods.

"We'll continue our exploration of the island," Colt said into his tactical microphone. "Same procedure as before and make sure you stay alert for any helicopter sounds. We'll take evasive action if we need to."

Chapter 35

In the Kremlin, Lev sat in his stuffed chair at the large mahogany desk in his office and looked at Yuri who was sitting in front of him.

"Our bosses don't want to use any helicopters from any branch of our Military," Lev said.

"Did they give a reason?"

"They want to maintain plausible deniability about the Kremlin being involved in any of this," Lev grunted. "If we use Military choppers, we won't be able to deny any involvement."

"We're using Poseidon Missiles. That's pretty obvious we're involved, isn't it?"

"Not necessarily," Lev said as his eyes flashed. "Ivan and Sergei are multi-billionaires and they're getting a lot of help from China who developed the version of the missiles they're using. It's plausible they could pull this off without any help from the Kremlin."

"Damn," Yuri said. "Isn't there something more we

can do to keep Randall and the taskforce from shutting us down again?"

"I think we can send Ivan a lot more of our top assassins."

"When are you going to check on that?" Yuri leaned forward. "We might not have much more time to keep Randall and his taskforce away from the Poseidon Missiles."

Lev checked his watch and then looked back at Yuri. "I'll check in just a few minutes and then I'll call Ivan and inform him of when he can expect some reinforcements."

"Are you going to request a lot of men?"

"I'll see how many they can send us," Lev said. "We have to make damned sure we stop Randall and his taskforce."

"Ivan has security devices installed in all his structures. That will help in being able to repel Randall, but getting a lot more assassins will help even more."

Lev nodded as he picked up his phone and punched in a number.

*****

In the main conference room in his headquarters in the archipelago, Ivan answered his ringing phone as he scanned the three other faces around the large table.

Sergei, Taras, and Yang stared back at him.

"My bosses don't want to provide any Military attack helicopters," Lev said. He went on to explain.

"We can't allow Randall to stop us again. We must launch the missiles this time."

"My bosses understand that," Lev said. "That's why they're going to furnish thirty more assassins to help you repel Randall and his taskforce."

"At least that's better than nothing."

"Remember, the Kremlin wants to be able to deny they had any part in this attempt to bring down the United States."

"The United States used some of their Military attack helicopters."

"That's a little different."

"How?"

"They knew they were being directly threatened by the Poseidon Missiles."

"How do we know that?"

"We have a lot of moles in Washington, and we can intercept phone calls too."

"We're being threatened too. Randall and his taskforce are over here on our soil."

"They're not on Russian soil and they're not threatening the Kremlin," Lev said. "Like I keep telling you, it's a different situation. The Poseidon Missiles that you control are threatening the United States, but Randall and his taskforce are not threatening Russia, Moscow, or the Kremlin. They're trying to eliminate a threat to the United States that you and Sergei are behind."

There was a brief silence.

"Okay, when are the extra assassins arriving?" Ivan asked.

"Within a few more minutes," Lev said. "I did manage to instill some urgency in my bosses. They're sending a group of their elite warriors who're training near you over there. Three of our patrol boats will be dropping them off on your island at a spot near where the missiles are located. I gave them the exact coordinates of the drop-off point." He went on to give more details.

"I'll have Taras meet them," Ivan said. "We'll use one of our patrol boats and get him to the drop-off point as quickly as we can. If the thirty new warriors get there first, get word to them to wait for Taras before they move inland.

He'll lead them to the places where we most need to beef up security."

"Yuri and I will make sure they have the instructions," Lev replied. "Good luck."

Ivan heard Lev disconnect and then looked at the three people around him. "You heard my side of the conversation. Now I'll give you the other side." He started explaining.

When Ivan finished explaining, Yang said abruptly, "I would like to go with Taras." He narrowed his eyes. "I need to be at the scene of the action. I must protect the missiles."

After a brief hesitation, Ivan replied, "Okay, both of you will go and you need to go quickly." He gestured to the doorway.

Taras and Yang rushed out of the conference room.

*****

After traveling through the woods for several minutes, Colt approached the next structure and noted it was probably another warehouse. He spoke into his tactical communications unit, "We'll use the same plan as before to check this next structure out."

"Roger," came multiple replies.

He moved toward the back entrance and waved everyone forward. The others followed in single file and stayed about five yards apart.

He checked the back door. It was locked.

Mack eased up beside him and removed a small kit from a vest pocket. He used a pick and in a few seconds, the 16 warriors eased cautiously through the doorway and looked for cover inside the warehouse.

While crouching behind some large crates just inside

the back door, they surveyed the huge room with a high ceiling and no windows.

About twenty rows of wooden crates dominated their view.

"Looks like the dimensions are the same as the last warehouse," he said into his tactical microphone. "Stay in your twosomes and we'll use the same procedure we used last time."

Everyone spread out along the width of the warehouse. Linda stayed with Colt.

Forklifts and other pieces of equipment were scattered along the floor among the stacks of crates.

Everyone moved forward.

"I see two people on a raised walkway about 30 yards in front of us," Colt said as he stopped behind a forklift. "Linda, move into a good position and target the one on the right, fire on my mark, three seconds."

She moved to a good position.

He gave a hand signal and started to count. "One thousand, two thousand..." He aimed his SIG 556 and fired.

Two soft pops sounded. One man fell to the floor, motionless.

"We got one, at least," Colt said. He and Linda rushed out from behind a forklift and ran a zigzag path toward the downed enemy combatant.

Alert for danger and keeping his SIG 556 in ready position, Colt charged forward, taking full advantage of various pieces of equipment on the floor to maintain maximum cover. Linda followed closely.

After reaching the downed enemy combatant who had fallen in plain view, he saw the other one had fallen on the raised walkway. Each enemy combatant remained motionless and had an obvious head wound.

He stopped behind another forklift and continued to scan the area.

"Another guy moving this way," Colt said.

"Where is he?"

"He's behind a crate right now, about 20 yards away."

"Can you get him?"

"I'm going to try. Watch my back."

"You got it."

Colt maneuvered toward the approaching figure. He had only gotten occasional glimpses of the man, but that was enough to know he looked Russian.

Giving the situation a little more thought, he decided he wanted to maneuver around behind the approaching Russian. He veered off on a cross aisle and then circled back.

Trusting his instinct honed from years of training and experience, Colt saw he had guessed right. He was behind his adversary.

He stepped out from a corner of the stacked crates and leveled his SIG 556 at the Russian assassin.

"One mistake and you're dead." Colt held his rifle steady.

The enemy combatant dropped his rifle and raised his hands in the air as he turned slowly toward him.

Staring hard at the man, Colt said, "Lose the pistol, left hand, two fingers. That's right. Now drop it and step away."

He whispered into his tactical microphone. "Linda, join me. I've got the one we spotted."

"Moving," She whispered.

Within seconds, she approached the two men and immediately moved behind the nearest stack of crates while scanning the area.

Colt glanced at Linda and the Russian moved with lightning speed unleashing a karate-style kick powered by his entire body.

When his rifle went flying, Colt realized Linda couldn't help immediately because of their relative positions. He was too much in her field of fire.

After the Russian's foot connected with Colt's SIG 556, the Russian was momentarily off-balance. Colt quickly stepped forward and slammed a forceful Karate punch just under his adversary's lower right rib cage.

The punch obviously injured the Russian, but it didn't take him out of action.

Snarling, the Russian bolted toward him and unleashed a straight punch. Colt moved to his right.

The Russian's punch hit nothing but air.

Colt immediately countered with a punch of his own that connected.

The Russian went down.

Colt dove at him, but he squirted away.

Gasping for breath, the Russian rolled toward his discarded rifle. He quickly grabbed it and swung the barrel toward Colt, who had sprung to his feet.

Reacting instinctively, Colt drew his Glock 19 from the holster on his right hip and fired twice.

When the 9mm slugs hit the enemy combatant's head, he immediately dropped. His AK-47 clanged on the concrete floor.

"Damn," Linda said.

Colt turned and saw two enemy combatants about thirty yards away who had come around a corner of some crates.

More Russians charged toward him from his right with their rifles pointed in his and Linda's direction.

The Russians fired, but the bullets missed.

It was the only chance they got. Linda (aiming her SIG 556) and Colt (still holding his Glock 19) fired multiple times.

All enemy combatants sagged to the ground and remained motionless. They were obviously dead.

Linda glanced at Colt. "Guess they thought they'd surprise us."

A slight grin flickered across Colt's face. "We aren't that easy to surprise."

Linda returned the grin.

Proud he and Linda were quite a talented twosome, Colt felt a new surge of confidence as he retrieved his SIG 556.

He spoke into his tactical microphone, "Status?"

The rest of the taskforce in the warehouse reported having successfully disposed of several dozen more of the enemy. They all reported being all the way down to the front wall.

Feeling a high level of urgency to find the missiles, Colt quickly left two men to secure the warehouse and moved outside.

Now having fourteen in his remaining taskforce, Colt continued toward the north as he punched a digit on his secure satellite phone.

He needed to check with Grant. All the next steps they would take needed to be precisely correct.

*****

At the Tampa FBI Headquarters, Grant sat at the large conference table in his makeshift control room with Frank, Paul, Steve, and Nick. When his phone vibrated he looked at the caller ID and answered.

"You ready for a status report?" Colt asked.

"Let's hear it," Grant said.

"We just finished searching the third warehouse. We killed more Russian assassins, and I've left two men at each warehouse to keep them secured. They'll alert me if they have any trouble they can't handle."

"Our satellites are locked in on your relative position.

I'll check the area around you again." Grant studied a set of new satellite images on the wall monitors. "I'm looking at some infrared images, and I think I can tell you where a lot more enemy is congregated." He gestured to the other four men with him and pointed to one of the new images.

A startled expression spread across Frank's face.

"That's a lot of people," Frank said, "must be reinforcements."

Grant noted the other three also looked startled as he spoke back into his secure satellite phone, "Probably about thirty people are in front of you along the path you're traveling. We have some new images just in."

"What do you see?" Colt asked.

Steve punched Grant's arm before Grant answered and pointed at one of the images.

"From the infrared images we know a lot of people are close together. They're probably in some type of structure, might be where the missiles are," Grant said.

"How far are they from us?" Colt asked. He knew Grant had his exact position due to having the infrared images.

"Hold on a moment," Grant said. "That group of about thirty has split into two groups and one of the groups is moving north. That second group has stopped, probably at another structure. So, you'll now have a large group to contend with at two different locations."

"We'll be prepared for a couple of large reception committees. So, again, how far from us are they," Colt asked.

"The first group is a mile north of you. The second group is only about a hundred yards north of the first group," Grant said.

"They might have two different structures set up to work on the missiles," Colt replied. "That would make sense. It would be safer to separate them."

Grant turned toward Steve and Nick.

After conferring with Nick for a few seconds, Steve looked at Grant and said, “Nick and I think Colt’s right. They probably have the missiles separated, each one in its own hi-tech preparation building. Each building probably has a mobile launcher parked in it or parked just outside.”

Grant relayed the information quickly to Colt.

“Keep us posted on any changes,” Colt said. “We’ll continue north for now and we’ll be prepared for a lot of action.”

“Good luck,” Grant replied. “We’ll recheck all the current images thoroughly and I’ll be back in touch instantly if there are any changes. You always keep your phone in the vibrate mode, don’t you?”

“Right,” Colt said. “Don’t ever hesitate to call me when you have an update.”

Grant heard Colt disconnect.

Chapter 36

At his headquarters in the archipelago, Ivan sat at the small round conference table in his office and looked at Sergei.

"Randall and his taskforce have taken out three of our warehouses and eliminated a lot of our assassins," Sergei said.

Ivan nodded and made no comment.

Sergei stared at Ivan for a few moments. "Shouldn't we change our tactics and get more aggressive instead of playing defense so much?"

"Do you have something specific in mind?" Ivan asked.

"I don't have anything specific at the moment," Sergei said. "I just thought it would be a good general idea to keep in mind."

Ivan nodded slowly while he reached for his phone and punched a button. He heard Dmitri answer.

"Are we getting close to breaking into the Federal Reserve System?" Ivan asked.

"Very close," Dmitri said. "We just need to do a little more probing to ensure we'll be completely successful. We also need to take a lot of care to remain undetected."

"Do you think you have enough time to be as careful as you want to be?" Ivan asked.

"I think we have enough time to ensure we make no mistakes when we hack into the American monetary system and take all their money. If we're careful, we should be undetected and they probably won't know immediately their money is gone."

Ivan gave a short laugh. "I guess I won't argue with that."

"Pavel, Dong, and I have worked hard to formulate the best strategy," Dmitri said. "We're also going to use the supercomputer we have here to create some false trails for the Americans to follow if they somehow detect our intrusion into their monetary system."

"And the supercomputer we have now is?" Ivan asked.

"We're using a scaled-down version of the Sunway Taihulight," Dmitri said. "The one the Chinese have in their National Supercomputing Center in Wuxi operates at a speed of 93.01 petaflops per second."

"Does the one you're using operate at that same speed?" Ivan asked.

"We haven't taken the time to set everything up to get an accurate measurement," Dmitri said. "No matter what speed it is, we're stuck with it. We think it should be fast enough to do the job."

There was a brief silence.

"Can you tell me again what a petaflop is?" Ivan asked.

"Remember a FLOP is a floating-point operation in a computer," Dmitri said. "A petaflop represents a thousand trillion of them. In this case, we're talking about 93 thousand trillion operations in one second."

Ivan narrowed his eyes. "That sounds pretty fast. And again, why do we need a quantum computer?"

"Because a quantum computer uses a lot of atoms that can all function simultaneously," Dmitri said. "It's a million times faster than the best supercomputer on the planet."

Ivan again gave a short laugh. "Okay, I think you've refreshed my memory. I'll let you, Pavel, and Dong get back to work."

"We'll keep you informed," Dmitri said.

Ivan heard Dmitri disconnect.

Chapter 37

Colt and the other thirteen warriors who were in his current assault force stayed in single file with the usual spacing as they moved toward the north.

The warriors moved on a dirt road about ten yards wide through an area dominated by large overhanging tree limbs.

Mack led his team along the right side of the road while Colt led his team along the left side.

Colt noted the road displayed a lot of deep tire tracks which indicated some heavy vehicles had traveled that way.

Mack looked in Colt's direction, pointed at the tracks, and spoke into his tactical microphone, "Probably from the vehicles carrying the missiles to the buildings where they'll be prepared for launch."

Colt nodded and continued forward.

Everyone stayed on high alert.

Shadows stretched ominously around them, but no immediate threats were apparent.

Colt heard Mack's voice in his earpiece "Paul just informed me we have a Hawkeye in the vicinity."

"Know if the Hawkeye has infrared?" Colt asked.

"Yes it does," Mack said. "And the Hawkeye shows a group of people in the direction we're going."

"How many people and how far from us are they?"

"Six people about a hundred yards ahead. They're stationary at the moment."

"We'll take the necessary precautions." Colt waved everyone forward as he spoke into his tactical communications microphone, "We're going to have some company in about another minute. Keep your eyes on the trees up ahead."

"Roger," came multiple replies.

*****

The lead assassin looked at the five men around him. "When Colt Randall and the taskforce approach our position don't be careless and react too quickly but prepare to take them out according to plan."

The lead assassin stopped as several responses rang in his ear.

"Don't be overconfident. Remember, this Randall bastard is a fierce warrior," the lead assassin said as he kept his AK-74 in ready position and scanned the area along the dirt road. "We shouldn't underestimate the jerk no matter how anxious we are to get him out of our way. Even though we'll surprise them, we must be extremely careful."

*****

Colt carefully scanned the area ahead as he moved along the dirt road. Linda followed about five yards behind him.

As he moved forward, Colt alertly turned his head from side to side. There, to his left, he saw movement out of the corner of his eye. A figure swung an AK-74 in his direction.

Colt quickly aimed his SIG 556 and fired, got him.

Linda moved closer and gave him a thumbs-up as they continued forward.

"We're approaching some thick growth," Mack said. "They're probably in there waiting in ambush. I suggest we be very careful."

Colt grunted. "No argument on that."

The taskforce continued forward.

In a few seconds, several muffled pops sounded.

Colt heard Mack's voice in his earpiece. "We eliminated two of them on our side of the road. Each man has multiple bullet holes in his chest, no body armor."

Using extreme caution, everyone continued slowly forward.

A faint sound from the top of a tree about 20 yards in front of him got Colt's attention. It was just a faint sound, but it instantly triggered his internal alarms. His past experiences had honed instincts that he couldn't explain, but, nevertheless, they were there.

"Incoming!" Colt spoke quickly into his tactical mike as he dove behind the nearest tree.

Torrents of bullets buzzed all around, kicking up dirt along with various pieces of tree trunks and limbs.

"Everyone okay?" Colt asked after the barrage stopped.

"Affirmative," came multiple replies.

Colt looked around and couldn't see Linda. She had

stayed five yards behind him the whole time.

"Linda?" Colt asked.

"Yeah, I'm okay," Linda said. "Thanks for the warning."

"Well, at least we know there are more assassins in the trees up ahead," Mack replied. "Colt, how in the hell did you know they were getting ready to let lose?"

"I heard some faint sounds and somehow got a feeling a flood of bullets would be coming."

"I didn't hear any sounds," Mack said into his tactical mike.

"The sounds were probably closest to me," Colt said. "We all should stay alert for any movement among the tree limbs. It looks like at least some of them decided to climb trees."

"Roger," came multiple replies.

Looking out around the tree he dove behind, Colt scanned the area for a few moments, nothing. He scanned a broader area carefully, still nothing.

"Stay in your cover," Colt said into his tactical microphone. "We'll let them take the chances first."

"Roger," came multiple replies.

In a few more seconds, Colt saw a man slowly shift his position on a tree limb. He moved his rifle toward Colt's position.

Colt fired instantly. His silenced SIG 556 only made a soft pop.

The man fell straight down onto the dirt road. He didn't move. His head was bleeding.

Colt noted the man was obviously another Russian.

"One down from the tree limbs and one less to worry about," Colt whispered into his tactical microphone. "We'll wait a little bit longer before we move."

The rest of the taskforce again acknowledged Colt's command.

While he continued to scan the area, Colt's left hand

closed around the front grip on the barrel of his SIG 556, which he pointed in front of him, barrel upwards at a 45-degree angle. His right hand squeezed the pistol grip. His right index finger was snug on the trigger.

All was quiet for several minutes.

Colt continued to scan the area ahead for another five minutes and detected no activity.

"Guess it's time to move out again," Colt said into his tactical microphone. "Anyone have any objections?"

When no one commented, Colt gave the order to move forward.

Linda stepped out from the tree trunk she was behind and back onto the left side of the dirt road. She again stayed about five yards behind Colt as she moved forward.

As Colt continued forward, his mind flashed back to the many training exercises simulating these same conditions.

Two men popped out from behind some trees about fifty yards in front. Their rifles were pointed in Colt's direction.

Colt cut the first man down with one shot. Instantly training his rifle on the other man, he fired again—the man toppled backwards just as his companion had.

Neither enemy combatant had gotten off a shot.

"Two more down. All look like Russians so far," Colt said into his tactical microphone. "Looks like Ivan Titov loaded his defense with his countrymen. I expected to see a few Chinese."

He heard a muffed pop from Mack's side of the road.

"Yeah, the one I got over here was also Russian," Mack replied. "We're staying alert and continuing forward."

Colt constantly scanned the area while he picked up the pace and kept his SIG 556 rifle in ready position.

"We might have cleaned them out right here. Take cover for a minute while Mack and I check on that," Colt said into his mike as he continued to scan the area.

A few more shots rang out, but these were sound-suppressed shots. Colt figured they were from his taskforce members. In a few seconds he heard Mack's voice in his earpiece.

"We got three more of the bastards over on this side of the road," Mack said. "I think they just arrived. They were moving toward us at a fast pace. Everything over here looks all clear again."

"Okay, let's move out," Colt spoke into his tactical microphone.

He glanced at Linda. "Let's go. Give me a five-yard head start."

She nodded.

Colt moved back onto the left side of the road and moved forward.

Linda waited a few seconds and then followed.

In a few minutes Colt saw movement among the trees in front of them.

Two enemy warriors popped into view about fifty yards ahead with their rifles pointed in Colt's direction.

Keeping his SIG 556 pointed forward, he cut the first man down with one shot.

The second man had swung his rifle toward Linda.

She fired first.

The enemy warrior toppled backwards.

Colt spoke into his tactical microphone as he scanned the area and prepared for more action. "Everyone report status."

"It looks all clear at the moment over here on the right side of the road," Mack said.

After Colt received an 'all clear' report from everyone else on the taskforce, he ordered everyone forward again.

Chapter 38

At Boswic in Tampa, Harlan sat at the round conference in his office and looked at Jim.

"Two things are becoming increasingly clear: the President doesn't want to escalate this conflict by using the Military more broadly and the Russian leaders are trying to preserve their deniability by keeping their distance," Harlan said.

"But we've known for a while that two prominent Russian businessmen are very much involved in the conflict," Jim replied.

"The Kremlin can still deny they have anything to do with this." Harlan said. "At least the President gave us some Military support when we needed it, and he has them ready to step in if we don't get the job done up there in the area around the west coast of Finland."

Jim nodded.

"It's good he seems to fully understand the urgency of preventing the firing of any Poseidon Missiles from up there around Finland," Harland said. "He's just hoping we can do the job again."

There was a brief silence.

"I'm glad we seem to be doing okay with our current efforts," Jim said. "According to our latest report, Colt and the taskforce are making some real progress. As usual, Colt deserves a lot of credit for that."

"It looks like the Chinese are still heavily involved."

Jim leaned forward and asked, "Have you received any more specifics on that?"

"They're still supplying a lot of technology support, mainly scientists with a lot of expertise on the Poseidon Missiles," Harlan said. "I understand they've also supplied a few more assassins and are again improving Moscow's capability to hack into our Federal Reserve System."

"You've heard all this from Grant?"

Harlan nodded.

"Is he still getting his information from the same sources?"

"Grant told me he just received a lot of updated information from the NRO, NSA, and the CIA. He also mentioned the intelligence agencies had shared all the information with RAND to get the benefit of the additional analysis from RAND's leading experts on the various subject matter involved."

Jim narrowed his eyes. "Let's hope Colt and his taskforce can continue their success and put the Russians and Chinese out of business on all aspects of this situation."

"We know we all need to give this new challenge our best effort to succeed in preventing a huge catastrophe for us," Harlan said. "Any slipups on any of our efforts up in the area around Finland could result in a major disaster for the United States."

Chapter 39

In his headquarters in the archipelago Ivan looked across his desk at Sergei.

"Do you have any new thoughts about how we can eliminate Randall and his taskforce?" Ivan asked as his intense gaze focused directly on Sergei. "We need to do something that works."

"We've used a lot of assassins, but they haven't slowed Randall down."

Ivan nodded slowly. "That's why we need a better plan."

There was a brief silence.

Sergei narrowed his eyes and leaned toward Ivan. "Have you received an update as to their exact location?"

Ivan didn't immediately comment.

Staring at Ivan, Sergei asked, "Well?"

"They're only about two miles from the first missile

structure and they're still moving forward. We definitely haven't stopped them," Ivan said.

Sergei grunted and then looked at his watch.

"We need an update on Taras's and Yang's situation," Ivan said. "We don't know if they split up or stayed together."

"You're thinking one of them might be in each of the missile locations?"

Ivan nodded. "If either one of them can knock Randall off, that certainly would improve our situation." He gestured to Sergei. "You call Yang and I'll get in touch with Taras. We need to find out what they decided to do"

"Do you think Yang is keeping his phone on vibrate?" Sergei asked.

Staring at Sergei, Ivan narrowed his eyes and wrinkled his brow. "He should certainly be well aware that's standard operating procedure for these types of situations."

"I hope he remembers that."

"He'd better. I've explained that many times to all the Chinese who've worked with us."

Sergei shrugged. "Just being extra careful, I don't want to take a chance of screwing things up."

Ivan gestured impatiently toward Sergei. "Go ahead and make your call."

After watching Sergei pick up his phone, Ivan grabbed his phone and punched in a number.

"Hello," Taras's voice rang in Ivan's hear.

"Are you staying alert?"

"Yeah and I know Randall's getting close. One of my scouts just reported he's now less than two miles away and heading directly toward us."

"How many men do you have?"

"Fourteen and we're well positioned and in good cover. We should be able to stop them."

"Is Yang over in the other missile structure?"

"Yes, we thought it best to split up."

"Good luck," Ivan said. "Give me a report as soon as you can."

"Roger."

Ivan disconnected and looked at Sergei.

Sergei had also finished his call.

"I guess you found out that Yang and Taras had gone to different structures where they're working on the missiles?" Ivan asked.

Sergei nodded.

"Is Yang prepared to fight if Randall gets to him?"

"He assured me he was ready."

Ivan took a deep breath and exhaled slowly. "It looks like everyone is ready. We'll see what happens. We need some good luck this time."

Chapter 40

Colt and his taskforce moved cautiously forward.

It was likely they were moving into another ambush, Colt thought, and they would need to react quickly. They would need to be lucky too. Maybe one of the assassins would make a mistake and give away their position like they did last time.

"Get lower and stay alert," Colt said into his tactical mike as he crouched and moved cautiously along the left side of the dirt road.

Within seconds, Mack's voice echoed in Colt's ear. "I see some movement over on this side of the road."

"Everyone stop and take cover," Colt said into his tactical microphone. He moved behind the nearest tree.

In a few more seconds Colt asked Linda to move up beside him. They peered around opposite sides of the giant tree trunk.

"I see two people in the trees on our side of the road about fifty yards ahead," Colt whispered.

"Yeah, I see them too," Linda said. "They're still moving toward us. I have a clear view."

"Target the one on the right. Three seconds." Colt gave a hand signal and started to count. "One thousand, two thousand…"

Two soft pops sounded.

One man fell out into the road and remained motionless.

The other one fell back into the thick shrubbery.

Colt heard a lot more soft pops.

Mack's voice again sounded in Colt's ear. "We got a bunch of them over here on this side of the road."

"Hold position for another few minutes," Colt said into his tactical microphone. "When we think the area is clear, I'll give the command to move forward again."

"Roger," came multiple replies.

In about another minute, Colt spoke into his tactical microphone, "Mack, how's it looking over there?"

"Looks all clear, but we're staying alert," Mack said.

Colt gave the command to move forward again. As he moved out onto the edge of the road, he knew Linda would wait a few seconds and let him get five yards ahead of her again.

*****

The assassin selected a position about ten yards into the woods on the western side of the road.

He stood behind the north side of a tree with the largest trunk he could find and waited for Colt Randall.

Eliminating Randall was the most important thing he could do.

He peered south around the trunk and made his plan. He glanced at his watch and figured Randall would be coming in his direction very soon.

While he waited, the assassin thought more about how he was going to attack. He knew the skills Randall possessed were exceptional and he decided surprise would be his best weapon.

He figured Randall would stay close to the road and

would be slightly east of him as he passed by.

After giving the situation some more thought, he decided he would wait until Randall got close and then slowly shift his position to the western side of the large trunk as Randall passed by. Then he would shift around to the south side of the large trunk and shoot while Randall was still moving north.

The assassin moved closer to the trunk and peered around the eastern side of the tree. He figured that would give him the best view to spot Randall before he got too close.

He figured the taskforce members would maintain a distance of about ten yards between each other as they came toward him. He smiled. That separation would give him time to disappear into the heavy brush after he shot Randall.

The assassin continued to smile as he waited.

His plan was good.

*****

After he had moved about one hundred yards, Colt heard a faint noise to his left and slightly behind him.

He turned quickly and saw an assassin swinging his rifle into a better position to shoot at his target.

Linda fired multiple times.

When hit with the high caliber slugs the assassin dropped straight down and his AK-74 bounced on the ground.

The assassin was obviously dead.

Colt looked at Linda and gave a thumbs-up.

"He apparently was well hidden behind that massive tree," she said. "You walked right past him."

He nodded and gave a slight smile. "Thanks, glad you

handled it as well as you did."

She returned the smile as they both stayed alert for more danger.

"Guess he needed to get into a better position to get off his shot, and he needed to make a last-minute adjustment," Colt said. "Also, he apparently didn't see you coming up behind me. He had a good plan, but he didn't execute well enough."

She gave a short laugh. "That's the last error he'll ever make."

Colt heard more muffled pops on the other side of the road.

As soon as the shots stopped, he spoke into his tactical microphone, "Status report."

"We just knocked off five assassins along our side of the road," Mack said. "Looks all clear now, and we're ready to move forward again as soon as you give the command. It looks like we have them pretty well cleaned out over here."

After scanning the area carefully, Colt gave the command to move forward. "Let's keep going until we find another structure of some kind and then we'll consult with Grant and decide what to do," he said.

"Roger," came multiple replies.

Chapter 41

In McLean, Charles drummed his fingers on the large table in the main conference room at CIA headquarters.

He and Paul both looked at several wall-mounted monitors.

The monitors showed multiple satellite photographs of a broad area around where Colt and the taskforce were located. Nothing significant showed on any of the images.

The infrared capability on one of the satellites had a temporary malfunction and was being repaired.

Paul wrinkled his brow and looked at Charles. "Have you had a chance to study all the latest information from NSA, and the NRO?"

"Yeah and there're a few more things to think about now," Charles said.

Paul gave a short sarcastic laugh and then mumbled, "That's all we need, more to think about."

"Both the Russians and the Chinese have launched some new satellites. Our analysts think they all have infrared capability."

"So, I guess they'll be able to keep an even closer eye on the progression of the taskforce."

Charles gave a slow nod and again drummed his fingers on the table as he looked at Paul. "I hope Randall and the taskforce can again accomplish their mission and prevent any of these monster Poseidon Missiles from being launched."

Paul gestured toward the satellite picture on one of the monitors. "The consensus of all our analysts and all the analysts at NSA is that the missile launch still is going to be from the area our Mark VI patrol boats are anchored."

"Shouldn't we do more to protect the boats?"

"Remember each boat has an eight-man crew and they each have six mounted 50 caliber machine guns, if I remember correctly."

"Six is the correct number," Charles said. "That gives them twelve machine guns in total for the two boats. They're well camouflaged and they're anchored about a half mile from the concrete slab where we think the missiles will be launched. I think they'll make it okay."

Paul narrowed his eyes. "Grant is still the one responsible for keeping in close contact with the boat pilots and Colt, right?"

"He's the only one I've talked with relative to Colt's status. Why are you asking this?"

"I keep thinking we're missing something."

"Such as?"

Paul gave a slight shrug. "I'm not sure."

"You must have some idea about what's bothering you?"

"I can't quite put my finger on it yet."

"We know the taskforce is closing in on Titov's headquarters and also the missile work sites," Charles said. "We should be getting another update from Grant real soon."

Paul gestured toward a couple of monitors on the wall displaying live satellite footage of the island the taskforce was on. "Maybe we can find a way to help them some in their search."

"We have a lot of analysts working on that. You and I need to concentrate on the big picture and make sure we're not missing anything." He leaned toward Paul. "Something along the lines of what you were trying to identify just a moment ago. I'm told the analysts at NSA, NRO, and the FBI have now been through every detail multiple times, so have our analysts. I doubt we've missed anything."

"However, I don't think we can ever rule out more surprises. That might be the main thing bothering me."

"Trying to identify the next surprise?"

Paul gave a slow nod. "I think that's a good way to put it. If we're aware of more things they might do, we have a better chance to avoid any problems."

Charles narrowed his eyes and didn't comment.

"From the beginning, China has stayed in the background. The Russians are still trying to do that, and both countries have been throwing more firepower into this than we expected. Many different aspects of this could accelerate at any moment." Paul leaned forward. "I'm glad the President decided to give us a little military support. Maybe he'll decide to provide some more real soon."

Charles rubbed his chin. "I think it's best to let the taskforce continue to handle this. Getting more military support could be overkill at this juncture. Grant is fully capable of making the right calls and Colt is fully capable of making the correct on-the-spot tactical decisions. So far, the taskforce has handled everything well."

"Except for those stealth boats that were going to attack them," Paul said. "If the Navy hadn't provided the support they did, we could have lost our whole taskforce right then."

"You have a point."

Paul gave Charles a sober look. "We still have a lot of unanswered questions and that's bothering me. I guess that goes along with wanting to avoid more surprises."

"Should we call Nick in here to review all the relevant technology again with us?" Charles asked.

"I've been keeping him busy analyzing more of the

information we got on the intercepted phone calls," Paul said. "I told him I especially wanted him to find out more about their timing to use their quantum computer to hack into our Federal Reserve System."

"Yeah, that's something we can't forget about." Charles lifted his phone. "I'll call Grant and get his latest status report. Colt and the taskforce need to shut down several things real quickly or we'll going to have a lot of big problems in a lot of ways."

Chapter 42

In the main conference room of the J Edgar Hoover Building in Washington DC, Ken Johnson, the FBI Director, sat at the long table with Frank Hellman (head of the Special Investigation Unit for Domestic Threats), and technology specialist Steve Locket.

The three men studied several rows of monitors along two walls.

After a few moments, Ken leaned toward Steve. “You’ve been working closely with the CIA analysts, right?”

“Yes sir, Nick Wallace in particular.”

“And you think we’re sure about what’s going on?”

“Yes sir, we think we know what’s going on and we think if Colt and the taskforce can execute correctly, we can bring all of these latest threats to an end real soon.”

“Does Grant have all the latest information from all of you?”

“Nick and I have given him every bit of data we have.

And he assured us he would pass any relevant information to Colt immediately."

"Did Grant confirm he's still coordinating closely with Colt?"

"He told me they just had a conversation ten minutes before we talked." Steve glanced at his watch. "The taskforce should have all the intelligence data we've accumulated, and they should be close to the first structure that's housing one of the missiles."

Ken nodded slowly.

"And you still believe the group of analysts you've been working with has figured out the big picture correctly?"

"Yes sir," Steve said.

"What confidence level do you have about that?"

"99.5%," Steve said. "Not much in this world is absolutely certain until it actually happens, but I think we've done a great job of figuring out what's going on up there in the archipelago."

There was a brief silence.

Ken picked up his phone and punched a digit. "I'll check again with Grant. It's logical the Russian moles in Washington are keeping the Kremlin fully informed about everything that's going on. They're probably keeping Ivan Titov informed about many of our plans."

Frank nodded. "I think we can be sure of that, and I think we can be sure the Chinese leaders are getting a full briefing too." He looked at Steve. "How many analysts outside of the CIA have you been working with?"

"Over a hundred," Steve said.

"Yep, I'm now 100% sure a lot of information got out to some moles." Ken took a deep breath and exhaled slowly. "Colt and the taskforce need to give this their best effort in every way to succeed again. Time might be running out for us before Titov and Nikitin have their Tsunami Apocalypse Torpedoes ready to launch."

Chapter 43

In his headquarters in the archipelago Ivan put down his satellite phone and looked across his desk at Sergei.

"Lev just told me Randall and his taskforce are just a mile away from our first structure housing one of the missiles," Ivan said. "He mentioned we have a lot more eyes in the sky and a lot more infrared capability now."

"Do you have any new plans?"

Ivan narrowed his eyes and said, "No." He pursed his lips and stared at Sergei. "Do you?"

"Have you found out where Taras and Yang are?"

Ivan grunted. "Not yet. I've tried several times, but I haven't been able to contact either one of them."

Sergei clinched a fist. "That shouldn't happen."

"They might be too busy."

"Doing what?"

"Both of them could be busy setting a trap for Randall."

"They should still find time to answer the phone, especially if you're the one calling."

"They might figure they have no time to waste."

A brief silence ensued.

"Not having time to answer the phone just doesn't wash," Sergei said, "especially when it's critical to coordinate closely."

Ivan set his jaw as his gaze rested on Sergei "One thing I've learned during the last year is that you can't underestimate Randall. You can't overlook any possibility. If there's any way he can get you he will. I've preached that to both Taras and Yang."

Sergei shook his head slowly and didn't comment.

"I'll try again to contact them in a few moments," Ivan said. "There's another thing we need to talk about real quickly that you've been responsible for."

Sergei tightened his lips and looked at Ivan.

Ivan narrowed his eyes. "Are we ready yet to hack into the Federal Reserve System?"

"Dmitri told me they're almost ready," Sergei said. "He and Pavel have just completed probing all the financial safeguards the Americans have and they've developed solutions to bypass every one of them."

"Have you done anything to check any of that?"

Sergei gave a slight shrug. "I'm not sure what I could do, but they say they're almost ready and that's true as far as I can tell. I inspected their setup in the second missile structure a few hours ago and I asked a lot of questions."

"Did you like their answers?"

Sergei nodded.

"Are they also going to use the supercomputer as part of the overall process?"

"Yes," Sergei said. "At the same time the quantum computer is hacking into the Federal Reserve System, they're going to use the supercomputer to probe a variety of accounts all over the world that transfer funds to the Federal Reserve. They want to make sure we haven't missed anything."

Ivan narrowed his eyes. "Exactly how soon are they

going to start?"

Sergei looked at his watch and said, "Probably in less than an hour. If I remember correctly, they have a little more fine-tuning to do to make sure the supercomputer and the quantum computer are properly synchronized."

There was a brief silence.

Ivan reached for his phone. "You call Dmitri and Pavel and check on things, and I'll try again to reach Taras and Yang."

Sergei nodded.

Chapter 44

In Washington DC, FBI Director Ken Johnson waited at the large table in a conference room, along with his head of the Special Investigation Unit for Terrorist Threats, Frank Hellman, his top technology specialist, Steve Locket, and his agent in charge of the Tampa office, Grant Winston.

In a few minutes, CIA Director, Charles Andrews, arrived along with his head of the Terrorist Threat Investigation Unit, Paul Collins, and their top technology expert, Nick Wallace, who reported to Paul.

Just as the CIA agents were settling into their chairs, Boswic Executive Director, Harlan Pierce, Boswic Vice President, Jim Boxer, and Boswic tactics analyst, Blake Morgan, arrived.

"Thanks for coming," Charles said. "I thought we all needed to get together in one group and discuss our strategy from this point on. Wc must stay closcly coordinated and we can't make any mistakes."

"Ken and I left the Whitehouse a couple of hours ago," Charles said. "The President sends his thanks for our bravery and accomplishments so far and emphasized we need to finish the job as soon as possible. He reassured us he has substantial military assets in position to provide any additional backup necessary."

"We already know the Russians want to bring us down so they can become the world's leading military power. And we know China has the same idea, but they're even more ambitious. They also want to be the world's leading economic power," Charles said. "They both think that's their rightful place on the world stage."

"They should realize they can't both achieve all their goals," Harlan said. "Something needs to give. Only one of them can be the dominate world power."

"Right now, they have one mutual goal to bring us down and they're determined to do that," Charles replied. "We're in the way for both of them and we have to be eliminated as the leading world military power and as the leading world economic power." He scanned the faces around the table. "So, they're working together for the time being and we have to make sure we eliminate these latest threats."

"If they destroy our economy, they'll each hurt their own economy," Harlan said, "at least for a while."

Paul nodded. "I don't think they're thinking about that at the moment."

"I'm sure that's true," Ken said. "Both countries are obsessed with getting us out of their way."

Frank leaned forward. "I think they've decided they'll figure out solutions to all the other problems later."

Charles gave a short grunt. "Yeah, I think all that's correct and that brings us back to deciding what we're going to do right now to make sure they never have to decide how to divide up the spoils."

Ken gestured toward Steve and Nick. "We probably need to get their latest analysis about the strategy being used before we get into a detailed discussion about what our next step needs to be."

"Russia and China both certainly want the missile strikes to succeed," Steve said. "And they both want to destroy any ability we have to resist their takeover."

"We all know that." Harlan banged a fist on the table. "We have to stop them right now and make sure their plan fails."

Charles leaned forward. "That's why we're here. Our taskforce must take the correct actions right now and we have no time to waste." He paused. "And we all know we're not going to get a second chance."

"Do you anything in mind different than what we're doing?" Harlan asked.

Charles scanned the faces around the table. "Not yet, but we need to analyze what we're doing and be sure we're not missing anything." He gestured for Steve to continue.

"I think we can expect some more deception," Steve said. "We need to figure out some things to tell Colt to look out for."

Harlan gave Steve a quizzical look. "Don't you think Colt has already thought about those things?"

"Probably so, but it's best to come up with some things to mention to him," Steve said. "We think the Russian chess masters have been developing the strategy and remember after ten moves in chess, a tree diagram of options has around 170 million branches. Colt might need a little help on being aware of some things Ivan Titov might do."

Harlan glanced at Ken. "Is that the way you see it?"

"I think we need to make sure Colt is aware of everything we think might happen," Ken said. He gestured toward the row of monitors. "We have an advantage he doesn't have."

Harlan gave a slow nod.

Charles made a sweeping gesture toward Nick, Blake, and Steve. "Do any of you analysts have anything more you want to say about this before we move forward in our discussion?"

"I agree neither China nor Russia seems to be worried at the moment about how they're going to divide up the spoils," Nick said. "They've teamed up real well to try to take us out. That's their focus and that's their clear goal at the moment."

"We know Russia has supplied the original missiles and China has improved them along with supplying supercomputers and other advanced technology," Blake replied. "They've indeed teamed up real well to try to bring us down."

"We have a lot of information about the size of the warheads on both the new Poseidon Missiles," Steve said. "We can be sure they're both 100 megatons. If they hit their targets, they're going to do a lot of damage."

Harlan nodded. "We need to remember that one and a half megatons is the size of the bomb we dropped on Hiroshima and two megatons is the size of the bomb we dropped on Nagasaki. Each of them did a tremendous amount of damage." He scanned the faces around the table. "If either of those missiles hits us, we're going to have one hell of a problem."

"So where does all this leave us?" Charles asked.

Harlan grunted. "There's no damn way we can allow any Poseidon Missiles to be launched. If any of them ever get on their way they're going to be almost impossible to stop."

Charles pointed to the images on the monitors. "Our satellites with infrared capability give us the exact locations of three sites Colt still needs to visit. We're now sure one of them is Titov's headquarters and the other two sites each house a missile. I think Colt and the other members of the taskforce can figure out precisely what to do when they get to each of the sites."

Harlan gestured impatiently toward a large whiteboard.

"Okay, let's start working on what we're going to tell Colt to look out for. We don't want him to get any surprises."

Paul nodded enthusiastically.

After asking Steve and Blake to join him, Nick stood and moved down past one end of the table where the whiteboard was attached to the wall.

Nick began making a list on the whiteboard.

Steve and Blake took turns adding to the list.

After they had thoroughly discussed the list, Ken looked at Grant and asked, "Colt always keeps his phone on vibrate, right?"

"Right."

"Give him a call," Ken said, "and, if he's not too busy, tell him what we've been doing and what we're going to recommend to the President. He needs to know that. And ask him if his has any new ideas he wants us to research. We might come up with some things he needs to know more about for what he does later."

Grant hit a button on his phone.

Chapter 45

Colt felt his phone vibrate. He knew it was probably Grant calling and he spoke into his tactical microphone, “Let’s halt and take cover for a few minutes. I think we’re about to get some more instructions from Grant.”

Colt removed his phone from a pocket and answered.

He heard Grant quickly explain the reason for the call and then ask him if he had any new ideas about the challenges he would be facing.

“Nothing new, we think we have a pretty good understanding of the situation,” Colt said. “We’re getting close to our next target and, according to all the satellite information you gave me earlier, we’re pretty sure it’s one of the structures housing a missile.”

“I think we all agree on that. The next target after this next one will be the other structure housing a missile and then the third target will be Titov’s headquarters,” Grant replied. “The main objective right now is for you to avoid any unpleasant surprises.”

Colt gave a short laugh. “Yeah, we don’t want any of

those."

"I'm looking on my handheld device at some of our infrared images from the satellites," Grant said, "and they show you're about a mile from your next target."

"Thanks for the update. We figured we were getting close, but we didn't know the exact distance. You told us a while back to keep going north and that's what we're doing."

"I'll get off the phone and let you get back to work," Grant said. "I'm in Washington and we've been discussing your situation for a while. We'll continue to discuss it. If we can come up with some new information you can use, I'll get back in touch immediately."

"Roger."

Colt heard Grant disconnect and then he spoke into his tactical microphone and had the taskforce resume their march to the north.

In about thirty minutes, when he arrived at their next target, Colt called a halt and peered out from thick foliage at a large concrete structure.

Colt studied the latest infrared photography he'd received on a transmission from Grant and then dispersed thirteen members of the taskforce around the large structure.

"Got a plan?" Mack asked.

"Pretty much," Colt said. "Come over to my position. You, Linda, and I will scout the inside of the structure and then we'll decide how many people we want to come in and join us before we proceed."

In less than a minute, the threesome used extreme caution as they moved toward a back door.

Mack grabbed a toolkit from a pocket and removed a pick. In a few seconds, there was a faint metallic sound from the lock.

Colt pressed against the wall as he slowly eased the back door open.

The three of them used extreme caution as they stayed outside and peered inside the structure.

"No sign of anyone," Colt said as he looked at an empty room about twenty feet square and with a ceiling about twenty feet high.

It was a perfect cube, Colt thought.

The walls and the ceiling were a drab tan color.

A dark brown door decorated the wall straight in front of them.

"Could be a trap," Linda whispered. She looked at the ceiling. "Don't see anything suspicious right now."

"I'll go first and then we'll try the next door," Colt said. He entered the structure and moved cautiously across the room to the brown door.

After looking around for a few more seconds, Colt motioned for Mack and Linda to join him.

Mack again grabbed a small kit from a vest pocket and removed a pick. In a few seconds he had the next door unlocked.

Colt eased the door open.

This time the room was huge, and it wasn't empty. It was about thirty yards wide, and three vertical rows of stacked wooden crates stretched for about fifty yards toward the other side of the room.

The crates were larger than they had seen before. They were shaped like large cubes with each side measuring about six feet.

Horizontal aisles cut across the fifty-yard-long vertical rows every five yards.

Another door was visible on the far wall.

This door was red.

Colt wondered if they were mistaken about a Poseidon Missile being here and this was just another drug warehouse.

"What do you think?" Colt asked. He turned slightly and glanced at both Linda and Mack.

"It's a big structure," Mack said. "It could be both a drug warehouse and a place to prepare the missile for launching with an active warhead."

Linda nodded. "I agree with Mack."

"Okay, let's keep moving and find out what's here," Colt said.

The three of them eased through the doorway and looked for the quickest cover.

They crouched behind the end crate in the middle vertical row just inside the door. The three warriors surveyed the situation.

No threats were evident.

Colt spoke into his tactical microphone, "Linda, follow ten yards behind me. Mack, you bring up the rear and guard against any surprise attack from behind us."

"Roger," came two replies.

Colt bolted from cover and ran toward the red door. Linda and Mack followed.

When Colt got a little closer to the red door, he moved to his right and pressed against the stack of crates.

Mack and Linda maintained their spacing and followed Colt's example.

They saw no opposition yet.

As they continued to scan the area, the lights dimmed and then went out.

Everything was now pitch-black.

Colt held his SIG 556 in ready position with one hand and reached for his night vision goggles with the other.

The goggles worked.

After a few more minutes of studying the area and seeing no opposition, Colt decided to move to the red door.

"Some light coming from something," Colt whispered into his tactical comm unit, "to our right front." He started toward the light, gesturing for Linda and Mack to follow.

Linda kept the previous spacing.

Mack was behind Linda, following about ten yards

behind.

They continued toward the light, their boots giving a slight echo from contact with the concrete floor.

Within a few more seconds, Colt saw the light was coming from a small opening under another door. He moved closer.

This door was also locked.

Colt waved Linda and Mack up to his position beside the door.

Mack once again reached for his toolkit. He tried for several seconds without success. Turning toward Colt, he asked, "Any clue how to get in?"

"Might be the same setup we found in some situations down in Jamaica," Colt said. He took a penlight out of a pocket and scanned the walls. He soon found what he was looking for. He moved to a new position and put his feet on a couple of round spots on the concrete floor while putting each hand in respective small indentions in the wall above the spots.

There were some faint sounds and the door slid open.

"You figured it out," Linda said. "Good job."

They peered through the doorway. A long hall with bright light stretched forward for about twenty yards.

The three warriors removed their night-vision goggles and eased forward.

Other than faint sounds of boots scuffing on the smooth concrete floor, there was no noise.

Linda held her SIG 556 in ready position and followed ten yards behind Colt.

Mack stayed ten yards behind Linda.

At the end of the hall, Colt saw three more doors, one straight in front of him and one on each side of the hall down at the end.

Colt raised a hand for them to stop.

"They probably know by now we're inside and I bet they're waiting for us, planning an ambush," Colt said.

"What do you want to do?" Linda asked. "There are three doors and three of us."

Colt looked up toward the ceiling. He saw a small tube that was pointed directly at them. The small tube had a lens on the end of it.

"I think it's better to stay together," Colt said. "Stay alert and give me a few seconds to think."

Chapter 46

In his office, Ivan looked across the small round conference table at Sergei and then pointed toward one of the large monitors on the wall.

"Well, at least we know where Randall and two other members of his taskforce are right now," Ivan said.

Sergei narrowed his eyes. "What do you recommend we do?"

"Yang is in there with the group guarding the scientists who're working on the missile," Ivan said. "At least I was finally able to get in touch with him and Taras and find out what they decided to do."

"Colt has three different options to choose from. What do you think he'll do?"

Ivan took a deep breath and exhaled slowly.

After waiting a few seconds, Sergei leaned forward and looked directly at Ivan. "Well?"

Ivan made a dismissive gesture with his hands. "There's no way we can tell right now. We'll have to wait and see what he does. At least he's in an area where we have a monitoring system set up."

Serge gave a slight nod and made no comment.

Ivan looked back at the monitor and waited. "He'll probably open each of the doors and study what's on the other side of them."

"Do you think he'll be able to determine which way to go to get to the missile?" Sergei asked.

"I don't think there's any way he can," Ivan said. "We'll wait and see what choice he makes and then we'll decide what to do."

Sergei gave a slow nod.

Both men waited.

After a few seconds, Ivan's said, "Remember the supercomputer is also in that structure and Dong is supervising the group of Chinese scientists who're working on it."

"I'm glad we decided to put the quantum computer in the other missile structure."

"The Americans do have a few good ideas. It's best to not put all your eggs in one basket."

Sergei nodded.

"We need to deploy a lot of people between the two missile structures in case Randall and his taskforce get past this next wave of our defense."

"Yang is in that first structure as a safety valve," Sergei said. "Maybe he can stop Randall if the rest of our assassins in there can't."

Ivan narrowed his eyes. "We know Yang is one of the most skilled warriors in the world when it comes to close-combat. Maybe he'll be able to surprise Randall and put his skills to good use. However, one thing I've learned over the last few months is that you can't underestimate Randall. You can't overlook any possibility. If there's any way he can get you he will."

There was a brief silence.

"And we're going to use the supercomputer to probe a variety of accounts all over the world that transfer funds to the Federal Reserve to make sure we haven't missed anything, right?" Sergei asked.

"Right," Ivan said. "I hope we can still execute our plan before Randall and his taskforce wreck it" He slammed his right fist on the table.

There was a brief silence.

"I hope our defenses in that first missile structure can hold. Yang should give us an extra advantage," Sergei replied. "I hope we can execute well and give Randall a few surprises."

"We'll see what happens."

Chapter 47

After giving their situation some more thought, Colt changed his mind and decided they would form three different teams and simultaneously check out what was behind each of the three doors.

He spoke into his tactical microphone and gave instructions for everyone outside to join them. He would send the remaining CIA agents to check out what was behind the door to the right. He would send the remaining FBI agents to check out what was behind the door to the left. He, Linda, and Mack would check out what was behind the door in front of them.

When the group from outside arrived, Mack used his toolkit to open the three doors and, per plan, various taskforce members moved cautiously through the open doorways.

Scanning the area ahead, Colt saw stacks of metal crates scattered about the floor.

Forklifts and various other pieces of heavy equipment were in various positions among the crates.

The high ceiling had a lot of metal railing and some metal crates on the railing in several places.

Colt kept his silenced SIG 556 pointed in front of him, barrel upwards at a 45-degree angle—his right hand on the rear pistol grip and his right index finger snug on the trigger. His mind flashed back to his Delta Force experience and the more recent training exercises.

He was well trained for this type of environment inside a building. He moved forward and prepared for a split-second reaction.

Two enemy combatants, rifles pointed down toward Colt, appeared in a raised area about twenty feet high to his left.

Colt cut the first man down with one shot.

The man fell forward, his rifle clanging on the metal railing.

While swinging his rifle toward the other man, Colt heard some more soft pops. Before he could fire, the other man toppled forward and down to the concrete floor, hitting it with a loud thud.

Linda and Mack had reacted almost as fast as Colt had.

Neither enemy combatant had gotten off a shot.

Colt gave a thumbs-up and the three of them kept scanning the area, including the overhead walkway. Colt continued to keep his SIG 556 in ready position.

After scanning for a few seconds and not seeing any more threats, Colt, while the other two stayed on guard, picked up a crowbar lying nearby and pried open the side of one of the metal crates.

A wide variety of small gadgets were inside.

"I guess this is a storage area for some of the spare parts they might need for various pieces of equipment," Mack said.

Colt and Linda both nodded.

After scanning the area again, the threesome moved forward, using extreme caution.

Mack glanced at Colt and whispered, "Don't like this, too quiet."

Colt nodded as he crouched lower. Mack and Linda did the same.

Within a few more seconds, Colt said, "We need to keep moving. We must find the missile they have in here and make sure it doesn't leave the building."

After encountering no threats for a couple of minutes, Colt waved the three of them behind some more metal crates and said, "We haven't received any reports, but I think it's about time to check the status of the other two groups." He looked at Mack. "You check with the CIA agents and I'll check with the FBI agents."

Mack nodded as both of them activated their tactical microphones.

"FBI group, what's your status?" Colt asked.

"We've been moving through a large storeroom," an agent said. "We've eliminated six assassins, but things are calm at the moment. We're still moving forward. We didn't give you a report because we figured you might be too busy. We figured you'd contact us when you were ready."

"That's good thinking," Colt replied, "any injuries?"

"No."

"Good, contact us if you come across something big we need to know about immediately otherwise we'll get back to you at various times for a status report."

"Roger."

Mack spoke into his tactical microphone and the CIA agents reported they were also in a storeroom, and they had eliminated four assassins.

None of the CIA agents had been injured and Mack told them to follow the same instructions Colt had left with the FBI agents.

"So far so good, let's hope we can keep it up," Linda said.

They continued on, slower now. Scanning the area with care, they moved forward through the storage room and toward another door.

This door was also red, and it was at the end of an aisle that ran between two long vertical rows of stacked metal crates. One horizontal aisle was obvious about halfway down the vertical aisles.

Colt, flashing a quick glance at Mack and Linda, unsnapped the leather strap over his Glock 19 and patted the handle of his pistol.

Concurring with the extra preparation, Linda and Mack nodded and also unsnapped the leather strap over their Glocks.

"It's smart to keep all of our defensive options on ready," Linda said as the three of them continued to scan the entire area, especially the area between them and the red door.

Colt's internal alarms alerted him as he continued toward the red door which was still about twenty yards away.

In a few moments, Colt saw a hulk of a man ease around the corner of a stack of crates ahead. The man, obviously Chinese, took a few steps toward him and then quickly ducked behind a gap in the stacks of crates.

The man was now hidden again.

Colt also jumped behind a gap between the stacks of crates. He quickly activated his tactical communications unit and said, "We have some company. He looks Chinese."

Mack and Linda also moved into some gaps between the stacks of crates.

"I got a quick glimpse," Colt said. "He looks well over six feet tall and he's a mountain of muscle. Also, he looks like he's over 400 pounds. I didn't see a weapon."

A brief silence ensued.

"He might be another one of those Chinese monsters who loves hand-to hand combat," Colt added.

Linda and Mack both responded that they also had gotten a glimpse of the assassin, and they agreed with

Colt's description of his size.

Linda and Mack also mentioned they didn't see a weapon either.

Everyone stayed in their position for another minute.

"We need to confront the Chinese assassin," Colt said. "I'll move forward and lead the attack. Prepare to back me up as is necessary.

"Roger," came two replies.

Within a few more seconds, Colt, using a lot of caution, came out from cover and moved toward the location of the huge assassin.

Keeping his SIG 556 in ready position, Colt took a deep breath and exhaled slowly as he prepared for some strenuous action.

Chapter 48

In his headquarters in the archipelago, Ivan disconnected from his phone call and looked across the huge mahogany desk in his office at Sergei.

"How much of my conversation did you understand?" Ivan asked.

"I knew you were talking to Yang. Because I couldn't hear his side of the conversation, I didn't follow many of the details of what you were discussing."

"You know we have surveillance devices all over the place in the structure he's in, right?"

Sergei gestured toward some of the monitors on the wall. "I've been following Randall since he's been in there and I've been watching the other members of Randall's taskforce too."

"Were you watching what Yang was doing?"

Sergei shook his head. "I've been concentrating on Randall and his group. That's who I'm concerned about."

Ivan leaned forward. "Well, I've been paying a lot of attention what Yang has been doing. I think he's our best chance to get rid of Randall."

"I heard you ask him some questions and then wish

him luck."

"He's getting ready to eliminate Randall. He gets the same images from our surveillance system as we do, and he knew Randall was coming in his direction." Ivan gave a slight shrug. "Now he's getting ready to eliminate him."

"Is he using his AK-74?"

Ivan grunted. "I tried to talk him into using it, but he wants to eliminate Randall with his bare hands."

"Why?"

"It's a passion with him and he's stubborn." Ivan shook his head slowly. "He told me this is what he's trained for, and he wanted to have some really great fun. He emphasized this was a chance in a lifetime for doing exactly that, having some really great fun."

"That's foolhardy. Randall will use his rifle and kill him."

"Maybe not," Ivan said.

Sergei looked curiously at Ivan.

"He thinks Randall will see that he's unarmed and won't shoot him."

Sergei shrugged. "Then Randall will keep his rifle trained on Yang and will take him captive."

"Yang doesn't plan to follow all of Randall's instructions. He'll wait for a good chance to take Randall out with his hands. One good blow from Yang should do the job easily." Ivan looked directly at Sergei. "If we can keep Randall from interfering, we should be able to get both missiles back on their launch vehicles and get them started toward the launch area within a couple of hours."

"Shouldn't we get some backup for Yang in case he doesn't succeed?"

"The American taskforce has already eliminated all of our other assassins in that structure."

"We still have Taras over in the other missile structure, don't we?"

"Yes and I want him to stay there and protect the other

missile. We want to be able to launch at least one of them."

"Have you made a request to Lev and Yuri for some more assassins?"

"A few hours ago," Ivan said. "He told me that he and Yuri would work on it." Ivan glanced at his watch. "I expect to hear back from him soon."

"Did he sound optimistic about getting some more?" Sergei asked.

Ivan shrugged and said, "Hard to tell." He looked again at his watch. "We should be finding out his results real soon."

After a few seconds, Ivan looked at Sergei and asked, "Are you keeping up with the details about what Dmitri and Pavel are doing?"

"They're close to being ready to start the hacking."

"How close?"

"Real close, I'm going to check with them again in ten minutes. I expect them to be in progress or at least be ready to start."

Ivan nodded slowly and then asked, "Is Dong helping?"

"I just checked with him, and I know he's been back and forth between the two missile structures. He's still trying to expedite everything he can in the areas where the Chinese scientists are working on the missiles," Sergei replied. "Maybe we can be ready to launch even quicker than what you mentioned a few minutes ago."

"I'm sure he's doing as much as he can," Ivan said. "He's a leading expert on the missiles and he might have some good ways to get the Chinese engineers to move things along a little more quickly."

Sergei gave a slow nod. "That's the mission I gave him when I sent him out there."

"When you talked with him, did you find out if Pavel had finished the troubleshooting for the entire computer hacking software with Dmitri?" Ivan asked.

"Yes I did and they finished that over an hour ago, why do you ask?"

Ivan gave a wry smile and then shrugged. It was just something I thought about," he said. "We have a lot of things going on and a lot of details to keep up with."

"There's another detail we might consider," Sergei said. He narrowed his eyes and stared at Ivan.

Ivan raised an eyebrow and waited.

"If Pavel and Dmitri are ready to start the hacking, we might let them wait a few more minutes while they go check on what Dong is doing."

"Are you talking about offering some advice to him?" Ivan asked, "Or just forming an opinion about what he's been doing?"

Sergei shrugged. "Maybe both, it never hurts to take some extra precautions when you're doing something this important."

"We know the Chinese aren't always forthcoming about everything," Ivan said slowly, "probably a good idea to get their opinion before we talk to Dong again."

Sergei picked up his phone, hesitated, and then looked at Ivan, "I think it would be better for you to call them."

Ivan narrowed his eyes and looked at Sergei, but he didn't comment. After a delay of a couple of more seconds, he slowly picked up his phone and punched a button.

When he heard Pavel answer, Ivan asked, "Are you and Dmitri all setup to start the hacking?"

After he listened to Pavel for a few seconds, Ivan said, "Good, now Sergei and I want you and Dmitri to wait a few minutes before you start the hacking process on the quantum computer and go talk with Dong about the status of the missiles."

"Do you have anything specific in mind?" Pavel asked.

"It's mainly to get an accurate picture of what's happening with preparing the missiles," Ivan said, "he's been talking with the Chinese scientists at both missile structures."

"Okay."

"But if you want to offer him any suggestions, you might do that."

"To help speed things up?" Pavel asked.

"That would certainly help. Getting the missiles launched properly is still our number one priority."

"Is Randall getting close?"

"He and his taskforce are in the first missile structure and will probably get to the missile in less than an hour if Yang doesn't stop them, so get moving."

"Do you know if Dong has gone back to the room housing the supercomputer?"

"We know he was there a few minutes ago."

"Okay we're heading out toward the first missile structure now."

Ivan disconnected and looked at Sergei. "Pavel told me everything is ready for the quantum computer to start the hacking. He and Dmitri can kick off the hacking attempt into the Federal Reserve System as soon as they get back."

Sergei gave a thumbs-up.

Ivan started to say more when his phone rang. He looked at the caller ID. It was Lev and he answered.

"Yuri and I both argued with our superiors a bit and we got some results I think you'll like," Lev said.

Ivan didn't say anything while he waited for Lev to continue.

"You're getting some more assassins and they're on their way over there. You can expect them to arrive within another hour."

"All Russian?"

"Some of our best and you're also getting another Chinese monster like Yang."

"How can he get here so soon?"

Lev gave a short laugh. "He was over here training with a group of our assassins. Our bosses decided to leave that whole group together to facilitate communication."

"That's all good news," Ivan said, "thanks."

"And there's more good news."

"Oh?"

"You're getting a tank, it's a German Panzer tank from World War II, but it's still in good operating condition."

"Did our President approve that?"

"He still emphasized he wanted to avoid another world war, but he figured you needed a little more firepower than you currently have. You and Sergei are both billionaires and this tank can be regarded as a bit of a relic that the two of you might want to buy. As a worst-case scenario, he thinks he can blame you and still maintain deniability."

"And you say the tank is in good operating condition?" Ivan asked.

"Long story short, we were doing some statistical benchmarking with our newest tanks and as a routine exercise our Military periodically uses a lot of other tanks to compare against. We just finished putting this tank through a lot of testing with live firing."

"Are there some shells left?"

"We're sending twelve over with it along with two of the pilots who're experts on every aspect of the tank."

"Great!"

Sergei looked curiously back at him.

Ivan gave a thumbs-up.

"If Randall and his taskforce get past the first missile structure, they have a big surprise coming," Lev said. "The tank is coming over inside of a big cargo plane and it will arrive with the additional assassins."

"How are you going to get it over here to the island?"

"The cargo plane is also bringing a big float that's designed especially to move tanks across any significant bodies of water, don't worry about the details just get prepared to use it when it arrives. You and Sergei are still responsible for the tactics you use."

"We'll be ready," Ivan said.

"Good luck."

As soon as he heard Lev disconnect, Ivan quickly gave Sergei a brief explanation.

Sergei flashed a big smile, waved a fist in the air, and then pointed to one of the monitors.

"Yang's getting ready to attack Randall," Sergei said.

Ivan narrowed his eyes and wrinkled his brow. "I hope he can succeed without a weapon, but at least we now will have a tank as an additional backup against Randall and his taskforce."

Both men watched the monitor.

Chapter 49

Inside the first missile structure on Titov's island, Colt held his Sig 556 in ready position and continued down the aisle toward the red door. He had asked Mack and Linda to stay behind and guard against a surprise attack from the rear or the sides.

Moments later, the large monster stepped out from behind the metal crate he had moved behind earlier. He had an expression like a lion eyeing his next meal.

Colt pointed his Sig 556 directly at the monster. "Any further movement and you die on the spot".

The monster flashed a big grin and stopped. He stayed completely still and he didn't seem to be worried.

Keeping his rifle pointed toward the monster, Colt moved closer.

"My name is Yang," the monster said with a big smile. "You might have heard of me."

"No, but you'd better follow my instructions if you want to continue living." Colt kept his rifle pointed toward the monster who was now only about five yards in front of him.

Colt stopped. He knew from past experience not to get too close.

Standing motionless, Yang glared at Colt. "I know who you are Randall and you have this all wrong. You're the one who's going to die. It's not going to be me."

"I might have a different opinion about that." Colt kept his SIG 556 trained on Yang, who reminded him of a huge beast ready to pounce. Colt had a strong urge to shoot him right there and be done with it. He knew the chance he was taking.

Yang continued to grin.

"Put your hands straight up slowly and then stay motionless," Colt said.

Yang didn't make any movement.

"I told you to put your hands straight up." Colt took a step closer and pointed his rifle at Yang's head.

Yang again didn't respond to the command. He made no comment and continued to grin.

"Did you know someone named Ho Cham?" Colt asked.

"I used to train a lot with him." Yang gave a short laugh. "I beat him every time. I'm the best fighter on this planet." He laughed again and bolted forward with lightning speed. He launched a karate-style kick at Colt's rifle.

The rifle went flying.

Yang lunged and swung a huge fist toward Colt's head.

Colt made a quick move to the side and avoided the blow.

Yang's momentum propelled him past Colt and onto the floor. But he regained his feet in an instant.

Both men stood motionless and stared at each other. Not seeming perturbed in any way, Yang continued to grin.

Colt prepared for another charge from Yang. He felt like he had one big advantage, he was quicker than Yang.

He backed off a few yards and quickly reviewed his strategy. He needed to figure out a way to gain more advantage.

Deciding some offense might work, Colt rushed forward, faked some moves, and then unleashed a furious kick, targeting Yang's right leg just below the kneecap.

Yang dipped down and to his left just at the right time.

Colt still managed to deliver a glancing blow. But being deflected, Colt landed off balance and rolled on the floor. However, he bounced back to his feet quickly and dropped into a combat fighting stance, feet spread about shoulder-width, one foot slightly forward.

Yang again went on the offensive. He seemed to still think he was the better man.

Colt felt a huge surge of adrenalin as the huge monster charged directly toward him.

Yang launched a barrage of vicious punches and kicks.

None hit Colt, who quickly dodged all of them.

Yang launched more kicks. All missed.

Colt felt a degree of satisfaction as he contemplated what to do next. He was six feet two inches tall and 225 pounds of solid muscle. He wasn't a small fry. He should be able to put up a good fight.

Both men backed off a little and did some heavy breathing. The last minute had been super strenuous.

Yang now looked irritated, good sign, Colt thought.

Colt backed off further and stood in an Aikido defense posture, facing his opponent with his hands open and in front, just above his waist.

"It's time for you to die." Yang let forth a huge growl and charged forward. He again unleashed a furry of kicks and punches. His last kick toward Colt's right knee partially connected and Colt staggered backwards, lost his balance, and dropped to the concrete floor.

Colt rolled on the floor and tried to quickly bounce back up. He felt a lot of pain in his right knee and he had difficulty standing.

After the huge effort he had put into the kick, the monster's momentum had driven him about ten feet forward and he had ended up with his back toward Colt and a little unstable after his last kick.

Colt continued to try to regain a standing position. He was still having trouble.

After he fully regained his balance, Yang turned toward Colt and crouched slightly to begin another charge.

Making a huge effort and putting most of his weight on his left knee, Colt managed to stand.

Colt's right knee throbbed as he put more weight on it. I'm in some trouble now, he thought, as Yang began his charge. He braced as best he could to contend with the oncoming monster.

Four soft pops sounded from behind Colt and a little to his right.

Yang slowed and staggered a bit.

Colt glanced back and saw Linda with her Sig 556 pointed at the huge monster. She had a determined look on her face as she spoke into her tactical microphone, "Good thing I came to check on you."

Colt took a deep breath as he turned and looked forward again.

Yang growled and charged toward Linda.

Linda fired six more times in the next second.

Yang fell forward on the concrete floor. He immediately began shaking and thrashing around.

Linda aimed carefully and fired two more times.

Yang continued to have a few convulsions, but otherwise he stayed motionless.

Linda looked at Colt. "There's no way you could have defeated this monster in hand-to-hand combat."

"I did okay for a while," Colt said as Mack walked up. All three stayed alert and continued scanning the area.

Linda gave a short laugh. "Whatever you think you

learned during your fight with Ho Cham, it wasn't doing you much good."

"I think Linda has a good point," Mack said. He looked directly at Colt. "We always need to stick to our rule of always shooting these types on sight. You're the best fighter we have in hand-to-hand combat, but you're no match for this monster." He gestured toward Yang who was now lying still on the concrete floor."

Okay I think each of you has made your point," Colt said. "I'll shoot the next one on sight. Thanks for stepping in when I needed help."

Mack and Linda each gave a thumbs-up as the three of them continued to scan the area.

Everything appeared to be all clear.

Colt spoke into his tactical mike, "Team leaders, what's your status?"

"We're in a giant storeroom and we've encountered no more assassins," one team leader said. "We have another door straight ahead."

"Same here," the other team leader replied.

"Keep checking things and we'll figure out how to get back together real soon," Colt said.

"Roger," came a couple of replies.

Colt looked at Mack and Linda and then pointed to the red door. "Let's see what's in the next area." He waved the three of them forward.

Chapter 50

In Tampa, in the main conference room at the FBI headquarters, Grant looked across the table at the contingent from Boswic. Harlan, Jim, and Blake sat across from him.

"I'm glad the three of you have a little more time to spend on discussing the situation in the archipelago," Grant said.

The threesome from Boswic all nodded.

"We try not to call Colt or Linda directly unless we have something extremely important to tell them," Harlan said, "something that will affect their welfare." He looked at Grant. "So, we depend on you to keep us updated on all the details."

"Speaking of details, I just got an update." Grant reached for a sheet of paper that had just emerged from a machine in the middle of the table. "I received some information from NSA when we arrived at the airport, and I needed to come here to use some special equipment to fully decode the message." He looked at Harlan and smiled. "Glad you could join me. There are several advantages to our being face to face."

Grant took about a minute to silently read the piece of paper he held in his hand.

"What's the information?" Harlan asked gruffly.

Grant narrowed his eyes. "The President has agreed to use a few more military resources to help us out."

"What's going on?" Harlan asked.

"Ivan Titov is getting a tank, a German Panzer tank from World War II," Grant said.

Harlan narrowed his eyes. "How did we find that out?"

"NSA intercepted a lot of phone calls," Grant said. "A couple of the calls were to Russian moles in Washington DC. Things were explained in detail on those calls."

"So Titov is about to receive the German Panzer Tank in the next few hours or so?" Jim asked.

Grant nodded.

"Have you told Colt yet?" Harlan asked.

Grant looked at his watch. "I figure he's real busy right now. I plan to tell him about the tank when he calls to give his next status report. He won't have to worry about the tank until he gets back out into the open and I'm sure he'll call before he leaves the current structure he's in."

Harlan gave a slight shrug. "Yeah, I guess your logic makes sense."

"I've never talked directly to the President about any of this," Grant said. "That's my boss's job up there in Washington."

"Except for giving us some extra support in special situations, the President is still going to stay in backup mode?" Jim asked.

"I think that's still the plan," Grant said. "If our taskforce fails, I'm sure he'll jump in full force. He knows we can't afford to let any of the Poseidon Missiles get launched, especially these new 100 megaton ones."

Jim leaned forward. "So, according to the content of the calls to the Russian moles, the Kremlin still wants to deny having any involvement with any aspect of what's happening up there off the west coast of Finland, right?"

"Right," Grant said, "and if not for the intercepted calls, they could make a pretty good case for that."

Harlan nodded slowly. "The Russian billionaires with their extensive wealth along with the help they're getting from China provide a good foundation for the cover up." He looked at Grant. "This whole thing was set up well by Russia from the beginning, using their chess masters to develop strategy, hiring the two billionaires to claim they acquired the Poseidon Missiles from China and then execute the tactics, asking China to partner with the billionaires and improve the functioning of the missiles……." He gave a slight shrug as his voice trailed off.

There was a brief silence.

"The Kremlin claims the Poseidon Missiles were stolen by a renegade group connected to China." Grant scanned the faces around the table. "Of course, we know that's not true, but it fits into a believable scenario with China stealing so much of the world's technology."

"We know both Russia and China are running all this behind the scenes," Blake said. "But they're both doing it in a way to properly maintain their deniability."

Harlan laughed. "They're not fooling anyone, but they are doing a good job of maintaining a foundation for their deniability."

"If we do too much while trying to stop them they can accuse the United States of starting a major war," Grant said. "I've been constantly assured by the Whitehouse the President will use a lot of Military force to stop a missile launch if he needs to, but he'll only do it if our taskforce fails. The FBI, the CIA, and Boswic must continue to cooperate closely, and we must make sure Colt and the taskforce succeed in their mission."

"Who's been keeping the President briefed on what's

going on right now?" Jim asked.

"Ken and Charles have both been doing that," Grant said. "Of course, they're depending on me to stay in constant contact with Colt and keep them briefed so they can give the President the latest and most accurate information." He glanced at his watch. "I'll need to call them again as soon as I talk to Colt. The President will have to make a decision on what Military resources he'll provide to eliminate the tank."

"Hasn't he already done that?" Harlan asked.

"Ken told me preparations are being made," Grant said. "He thinks the President will order using the same helicopters again that destroyed the stealth boats. This time they'll use bombs that are tank killers."

Harlan grunted. "That should work."

"I'll make sure Colt gets all the updates as soon as he calls." Grant looked at his watch again. "If he doesn't call within the next fifteen minutes, I'll give him a call. I don't want to wait very long before I tell him about the tank."

Chapter 51

In the J Edgar Hoover building in Washington DC, Ken stood and welcomed the three CIA agents from McLean into the main conference room.

Charles, Paul, and Nick settled into chairs across the large table from Ken, Frank, and Steve.

"You probably got the same message from NSA I did about the taskforce?" Ken looked quizzically at Charles.

Charles nodded. "I just got one. It probably was the same as yours."

"I wanted you to come over to review all the aspects of that news," Ken said. "One mistake by the taskforce could lead to some catastrophic problems, ones difficult to overcome."

"Did your message have them in the first structure that's housing one of the missiles?" Charles asked.

"Yes," Ken said. "It's a big structure and it has a lot of rooms, many of them storerooms."

Paul leaned forward. "Does Colt know about the tank?"

"I just talked to Grant right before you got here," Ken said. "He's expecting Colt to call in the next few minutes to give him a status report. Grant's going to give Colt the latest update then."

Charles looked directly at Ken. "And you've been talking with the President, right?"

"Right," Ken said.

"Is he going to get the Military involved again to take care of the tank?" Charles asked.

"Yes, and he'll probably use the same helicopters again that he used to destroy the stealth boats," Ken said.

Charles stared at Ken. "I hope we can pull it off okay. A Panzer Tank might be old, but it's still a powerful force, especially against a group without heavy weapons."

Frank scanned the faces around the table. "Can anyone think of something we need to tell Grant to relay to Colt?"

"We need to get all the specific data about our attack plan with the helicopters," Paul said, "and that should be passed on to Colt. He needs to have every detail about what to expect."

"I think we all know that," Frank snapped. "Is there anything else we need to make sure we don't overlook?"

After about five more minutes of discussion, no one came up with anything else specific that Colt would need to know.

"I think the helicopters that were used last time had a lot of hi-tech equipment," Nick said. He glanced at Steve.

Steve nodded. "The pilots should be able to locate the tank quickly and they should be able to communicate with Colt and the taskforce. It would probably be good for us to check all those details again and make sure Grant has them to pass on to Colt."

Everyone nodded.

Chapter 52

In Tampa in the main conference room at the FBI headquarters, Grant picked up his ringing phone while the Boswic contingent was still there.

"It's Colt," Grant said. He answered.

"What's your status?" Grant asked. He listened for about a minute, asked a few questions, listened some more, and then disconnected.

"They're still in the first missile structure," Grant said. "All the taskforce members are still okay. Colt's group is preparing to move into the next area." He went on to explain.

"So, they're still split up?" Harlan asked.

"The groups are the same as when Colt gave his last status report," Grant said. "Colt, Linda, and Mack are still together and getting ready to see what's behind the red door."

"That door being red could have some significance." Jim narrowed his eyes. "Did Colt mention anything about that?"

"He did, and he thought it might have some significance to the missile's location," Grant said. "I guess he's about to find out."

"Did Colt mention anything about how he's going to get his team back together?" Harlan asked.

Grant nodded. "He's communicating closely with each team leader. He thinks they'll all get back into the same area real soon. All the doors the other two teams have opened have led back toward the center of the complex."

"Does Colt know if any of the others encountered a red door?" Jim asked.

"Colt told me that both the other two teams have gone into areas that were behind red doors. He thinks the red doors all lead toward the area with the missile," Grant said. "That's the main reason he thinks all fourteen of them will get back together real soon. If they find the computer area first, Colt will dispatch some of the team to shut down the activity there. He and the rest of the team will continue searching for the area containing the missile since that's the most critical issue."

"Can't NRO use some infrared images and do something to help them in their search?" Blake asked.

"I was told they've been trying," Grant said. "NRO has been making multiple sweeps with their various reconnaissance satellites. The satellites with the infrared capability haven't been able to penetrate the ceilings in either of the missile structures so they can't locate where the people are."

"What about NSA?" Jim asked. "Have they been able to intercept any calls and determine locations?"

"NSA has several satellites with special capability in that area." Grant said. "They've been able to intercept several calls, but they haven't yet been able to pinpoint the exact locations of any of the callers inside that structure."

Harlan leaned forward. "Are all the callers up in that

area?"

"Some are there and many are in other places, even Washington DC," Grant said. "When we can determine a more specific location of each caller we intercept, we can put together a much more complete picture of everything that's going on. A lot of analysts are working on that."

Blake nodded. "I've been working with Steve and Nick on some of that. We've produced some useful results on several broader aspects of the situation, both in Finland and elsewhere."

Harlan slammed a fist on the table. "Finding the damned missiles is the most important thing right now." He looked directly at Blake. "Have you helped any on that?"

"Maybe," Blake said. "Right before this meeting, Nick, Steve and I sent our analysis of a lot of data collected from the intercepted phone calls to NRO and NSA." He looked back at Harlan and then at Jim. "I think we pointed out some things that could help both NRO and NSA, especially if they have some collaborating data."

Harlan nodded slowly and didn't comment.

Grant looked at the Caller ID on his ringing phone. "It's Charles." He glanced at Blake before he answered. "Charles wouldn't be calling just to chat. Maybe NRO and NSA put all that analysis you sent them to good use."

Blake signaled a thumbs-up.

Grant pushed the button and answered.

Chapter 53

In the first missile structure on Ivan Titov's island, Colt, Linda and Mack moved up beside the red door.

Before he opened the door, Colt said, "We're probably going to encounter one hell of a lot of opposition when we get close to the missile area or the computer area, especially if we're getting close to both of them." He eased the door open and peered into the next area.

"Another wide hallway," Colt said. He pointed toward three doors.

One was straight ahead and there was one on each side of the hall close to the end door. The setup was the same as they had seen in the last hall, the hall where they had split into three groups. The door straight in front of them was red.

The three of them moved forward and scanned the ceiling of the hallway as they went.

"Sure enough, there's a camera mounted up there," Colt said. He pointed toward it.

Mack and Linda both nodded as the three of them continued forward toward the doors.

Colt spoke into his tactical microphone, "Team leaders, what's your situation?"

"We've come to another red door," the first team leader said.

"Same here," the other team leader replied.

"I think when you go through them you're going to meet up with us again," Colt said. "So don't be surprised. We don't want to shoot each other."

"Roger," both team leaders replied.

In a few more seconds, the fourteen remaining members of the taskforce were reunited again.

"I don't like this," Mack said. "I think we need to move quickly."

"Agree, my gut tells me there's danger close around," Colt said. "Make sure you have your protective mask handy. You might need it."

Chapter 54

In his office on his island in the archipelago, Ivan looked across his large mahogany desk at Sergei.

"Well, we lost Yang," Ivan said.

Sergei nodded and said, "We haven't yet gotten any benefit from any of his type. They might be great in some cases, but they just don't fit into any of our situations."

"That's a point to keep in mind going forward," Ivan said.

"Randall and his taskforce are too alert." Sergei frowned. "They aren't easy to surprise."

Ivan didn't comment.

"Yang's type is a lot more effective when they can catch an enemy force by surprise. Most warriors can't respond very well for a few moments after they're surprised," Sergei said. "However, that's not Randall's weakness. In fact, it's his strong point. He stays alert and he responds quickly to any type of attack that's launched against him."

Ivan took a deep breath and exhaled slowly. “Well, we still have a good many surprises left for him.” He pointed to one of the wall-mounted monitors. “The next surprise we’re going to give him will be in just a few more seconds.”

Sergei looked at the monitor.

The monitor showed Randall uniting with the rest of his taskforce.

Sergei studied the image for a moment and then looked back at Ivan. “What are you going to do?”

“Give them a good dose of nerve gas.”

Sergei stared quizzically at his partner.

After leaning slightly forward, Ivan reached under the middle of his desk. He grabbed something and yanked it toward him.

Sergei saw a panel in Ivan’s desk being exposed.

A black button was in the center of the panel Ivan had grabbed.

Ivan pointed toward the monitor. “This will release nerve gas into that chamber Randall is in.”

“I didn’t know you had this installed,” Sergei said.

Ivan shrugged. “I had a lot of things installed at the last minute, but we’ve both been real busy. I haven’t had a good chance to keep you fully informed on everything.”

Sergei gave a quick nod and said, “Understood.”

“You ready for some fun?” Ivan asked.

“I hope that refers to getting rid of Randall and his taskforce,” Sergei said as he kept his gaze on what Ivan was doing.

Ivan looked directly at Sergei. “That’s exactly what it means. I think it’s high time we all said goodbye to Randall and his whole damned group.”

Sergei gave a thumbs-up as he narrowed his eyes and continued to watch what Ivan was doing.

Ivan displayed a big grin and reached for the black button.

"We can overcome not hacking into the Federal Reserve System, but if we fail to launch any missiles, our whole mission fails miserably." Ivan said.

Sergei nodded.

Ivan flashed a big grin. "I'm going to make sure none of Randall's group gets into the missile room and I'm going to do that right now."

Sergei leaned forward as he watched Ivan press the button.

Immediately both Sergei and Ivan turned back toward the wall-mounted monitor.

Chapter 55

In Tampa in the main conference room at the FBI headquarters, Grant picked up his ringing phone while the Boswic contingent was still there.

"Have you told Colt about the tank yet?" Charles asked.

"No, I thought it would be too distracting right now. He's right before trying to find the first missile," Grant said. "I'll tell him about it when the time is right, definitely when they go back outside."

"I have something else for you to tell him."

Grant waited for Charles to continue.

"We still have a Wasp Class Navy helicopter carrier up there in the north Atlantic area," Charles said. "It's an older one, but it has what we need."

"Which one is it?" Grant asked.

"The Navy won't tell us," Charles said. "I guess they're still concerned about some Russian moles getting the information."

"What good does knowing the name of the carrier do the Russians or the Chinese?"

"I'm not sure, but that's the way the Navy wants it."

"But they told you it was an older one, right?"

"They apparently thought we would figure that part out after they told us about the helicopters," Charles gave a short laugh. "And they were right about that."

"You think you know the name of the carrier?"

"We're pretty sure it's the Essex that went into service in 1992," Charles said. "It's carrying the older AH-64 Apache Helicopters."

"Do they have tank killer missiles?"

"Yes, they all carry Hellfire antitank missiles, and the choppers all have TADS."

"What's that?"

"It stands for Target Acquisition Designation System," Charles said. "And it can detect the heat given off by a tank from a distance up to seven miles. I was told they're already on their way to the archipelago."

"How soon will they get there?"

"They might be a little on the older side, but they can still fly at 227 miles per hour. They should arrive in the target area in about fifty minutes. When you talk to Colt, make sure he knows that."

"I should be able to give him the news soon. If he doesn't call in again within the next half hour, I'll call him. He always keeps his phone on vibrate when he's on a mission."

"That sounds like a plan," Charles said.

Grant heard Charles disconnect and then looked at Harlan.

"The Navy is going to eliminate the tank threat," Grant said. "They still have a helicopter carrier in the upper Atlantic that's not far from the area around Finland. AH-64 Apache helicopters using Hellfire antitank missiles will take care of things."

Harlan leaned forward. "I heard what you told Charles, and I think that's the right thing to do."

"I'll make sure Colt know real soon about the tank and the plan to eliminate it," Grant said as he looked directly at Harlan. "As is true with any project, things could always go wrong. He needs to take the right precautions just in case there's a problem."

Grant nodded. "No argument about that."

Chapter 56

In the first missile structure in the archipelago, Colt's fourteen taskforce members stayed alert and prepared to move forward.

Soon after Colt had warned everyone to keep their protective mask ready for use, something that appeared to be a thin mist started floating down from a vent on the ceiling.

Everyone donned their mask in less than a second.

Colt did a quick scan of the group around him.

No one seemed affected.

"How did you know that was going to happen?" Linda asked, glancing at Colt.

"Some combination of experience and intuition," Colt said as he moved toward the next red door and waved everyone forward. "I also knew we were in a hallway that might have been designed for eliminating an enemy force before they could go into the next area, which probably contains the missile."

Linda gave a thumbs-up.

Colt stopped at the door and turned the knob.

The door was unlocked and Colt eased it open. He knew they had to find the missile quickly and stop it from being launched. As more time passed, that was becoming more critical.

After scanning the immediate area, which was crowded with large equipment, Colt determined that things looked clear enough to enter. He moved forward and stopped behind the nearest cover, which was something like a large forklift.

Colt moved to the corner of the huge machine and peered around it. More large pieces of equipment blocked his view, but there was no indication of any opposing forces yet.

Colt spoke into his tactical communications microphone. "I've seen no opposition in here yet, so everyone come in cautiously, spread out, and use the best cover you can find. We check things out and then we'll decide what to do next."

"Roger," came multiple responses.

In a few more seconds, Colt saw Linda and Mack come quickly over to his position.

Everyone studied the area ahead. It had some equipment in a perfect line down the middle for about ten yards and then a brick wall blocked the view. There was about a five-foot-wide opening on each end of the wall.

Colt glanced at Linda and Mack. "What do you make of the situation?"

"As for as any opposition is concerned, I still don't see any," Mack said. He looked at Colt and then spoke into his tactical microphone. "Anyone see any people of any kind around?"

All replies came back negative.

"The ceiling extends a long ways past the brick wall, so we have a ways to go," Colt said. He looked at Mack. "I'll get my team together and lead the way. Your team will stay about twenty yards behind us and guard the rear."

"They're probably waiting on the other side of the brick wall for us to show up," Linda said. "There will likely be plenty of cover for them to stage an ambush."

Colt nodded just as his secure satellite phone vibrated. He deactivated his tactical communications unit and removed the phone from a pocket. He looked at the phone, and said, "It's Grant. I'm sure he wants a status report. Tell everyone to stay on alert while I take a minute here to brief him on our status."

Linda and Mack nodded and spoke into their tactical microphones.

Colt answered his phone.

"What's your situation?" Grant asked.

Colt explained.

"Okay, good," Grant said. "Now I have some interesting news for you."

Colt listened while Grant explained about the tank.

"Is there anything we need to do in that regard?" Colt asked.

"No," Grant said. "It's all taken care of. You might hear some explosions if you get out of the missile structure pretty soon, and we thought you would like to know what was going on. Good luck going forward."

"Thanks," Colt said as he heard Grant disconnect.

Colt looked at Linda and Mack and explained about the tank.

He reactivated his tactical communications unit and said, "Let's get ready to move."

In less than a minute, Colt and his group reached the brick wall and spread out around the area.

Mack kept his group well behind Colt's group to protect against any attack from the rear.

Colt and Linda went to one of the openings and scanned the area ahead.

As he examined the area in front of him, Colt heard a

lot of sound-suppressed gunfire in multiple bursts and in multiple areas.

All the shots were behind him.

Within less than a minute, Mack's voice rang loudly in the tactical communications unit in Colt's ear, "We've eliminated about thirty enemy combatants who came charging toward us from the rear. Guess they thought they could surprise us."

"Did you get all of them?" Colt asked.

"Think so," Mack said. "All of us back here compared notes. No one saw anybody retreat."

"We'll wait a few more minutes," Colt said. "If we don't have any activity, we'll move forward again."

After another five minutes, Colt stepped out from behind the wall. No one fired a weapon.

"Looks like we can move forward again," Colt said into his tactical mike. "But stay alert and continue to look around in case we have some opposition left in here."

"Roger," came multiple replies.

Colt waved everyone forward.

Linda stayed behind Colt and ahead of the rest of the taskforce. Everyone kept about five yards of separation.

Colt moved around more obstacles and stopped behind a big piece of machinery. He peered around the large metal object and saw the main thing he had been looking for.

A huge Poseidon Missile loomed before him. Even though he knew the dimensions, it seemed even larger than he expected. The nose cone of the 80 foot long and 8 foot wide cylinder was like that of a large jet, but it was much more menacing.

Colt had an odd feeling. It was something like having a sudden encounter with a large monster. He quickly shook off the feeling and concentrated on the situation.

Three Chinese workers labored feverishly over the missile sitting on what appeared to be a launch mechanism mounted on a transport vehicle.

Colt stayed behind cover and waved for Linda and Mack to join him.

"None of the workers have weapons," Colt said. "They seem to be concentrating hard on what they're doing, and they don't give any indication of knowing we're here."

Linda looked at Colt. "We need to stop them immediately, but we need to be cautious. There's a lot of heavy equipment around and we could have another ambush."

Colt nodded and spoke into his tactical microphone, "Everyone ease up close to my position and then prepare to charge forward. Stay ready to dive to the floor if you draw any fire. Mack, Linda, and I will take care of the workers."

"Roger," came multiple replies.

When all the taskforce members got in position, Colt stepped out from behind the large piece of machinery and took a few steps forward.

No one fired at them.

Colt waved everyone forward and they rushed past the missile and the Chinese workers while he, Mack, and Linda walked closer to the workers and pointed their rifles at them.

All the workers stopped what they were doing and raised their arms straight up.

"Does anyone speak English?" Colt asked.

None of the workers said anything. They all just stood there with their hands up and stared at Colt.

Linda glanced at Colt."Guess you have your answer."

Colt nodded as he heard the two leaders, who had taken their teams to check the rest of the structure, report that all was clear.

Due to the need to guard the workers as well as secure the missile and the facility, Colt left four men this time and led his remaining team of ten back outside to continue their mission toward the next missile structure.

Chapter 57

In Tampa in his office at the FBI headquarters, Grant reached for his ringing phone. He saw the call was from Ken and he answered.

"What's Colt's status?" Ken asked.

"He's secured the first missile structure and is outside moving toward the second one," Grant said. "They eliminated a lot of assassins inside the structure, thirty of them during one attack."

"Did we have any casualties?"

"No and I think that's amazing. Some of it might be luck, but I think a lot of it is due to Colt's excellent leadership. He's a master of a huge array of tactics in close combat situations."

"That's why Charles insisted he lead our taskforce."

"And I think we both agree with Charles, right?"

Ken gave a short laugh and said, "Right."

"Do you know the status of the attack helicopters?" Grant asked.

"Charles gave me an update about five minutes ago. There are two Apache AH-64 helicopters getting close to the island. They each have two Hellfire antitank missiles in case there are any surprises. They'll each fire one of their missiles to start with and still have a backup if they need to use it."

"And, if I remember correctly, they can identify their targets from seven miles away, right?"

"That's correct. Randall should be hearing some explosions very soon."

There was a brief silence.

"Do you know if Randall is keeping in close touch with the two patrol boat pilots?" Ken asked.

"I know he's been checking with them when he gets a chance, and I think that's fairly often. The last time I talked to him about it he mentioned the crews on both boats were staying on constant guard against an attack and were manning the four 50 caliber machine guns on each of the boats."

"Good."

"Do you know if the President is still going to send in a group of Marines to secure the area up there like he did down in Jamaica?"

"That's the plan and they should show up as soon as Colt completes his mission."

"What if Colt has a problem?"

"Then I think they'll show up sooner."

Grant went over a few more details with Ken before they ended their call. They had to make sure everyone stayed closely coordinated. This mission was as critical as the one in Jamaica, maybe even more critical.

Chapter 58

Ivan sat in the main conference room in his headquarters on his island in the archipelago and looked across the large table at Sergei. He had decided to move to the conference room because it had a lot more monitors than his office. He pointed to one of the wall-mounted monitors.

"They're on their way to the next missile structure," Ivan said. "I hope the tank can stop them."

"We both keep saying you can't underestimate Randall. We know we can't overlook any possibility. If there's any way he can get us he'll take advantage of it"

Ivan nodded. "Yes he will, but now we have a tank, and I don't think his taskforce is equipped to fight it." He narrowed his eyes and leaned toward Sergei. "I think we now have a weapon Randall won't be able to stop."

"Randall is a master at tactics. He somehow anticipated our trap and got his whole team through our improvised gas chamber."

"They obviously have good protective masks, and they

must also have some very protective clothing. That was some strong nerve gas we used."

Sergei pursed his lips and didn't comment.

"I'll check again with Taras on the situation in the second missile structure. I'll let him know Randall and his taskforce are coming that way just in case the tank doesn't stop all of them."

"Does Taras know about the tank?"

"I briefed him on it as soon as I found out."

Sergei nodded slowly and didn't comment.

Ivan grabbed his phone and stabbed a button hard with his forefinger. He heard Taras answer.

"Randall and his taskforce took over the first missile structure and they're heading in your direction," Ivan said. "I wanted to make sure you were aware of that."

"I'll make sure he doesn't succeed here. Hell, I'll stop him myself if I need to."

Ivan asked, "Is the missile ready to send to the launch site?"

"Pavel and Dmitri just inspected it. They have the Chinese workers making a few more adjustments. They told me they'll be back in a few minutes to inspect it again. They said it was almost ready."

Ivan grunted. "We need to hurry. Maybe I should call them and get more details."

"I asked a lot of questions and got a lot of answers. They assured me everything is being done as fast as possible. They told me to have some patience and that it will do us no good to launch and have a malfunction."

Ivan grunted again and didn't comment.

A brief silence ensued.

Ivan narrowed his eyes as he spoke. "Our chess masters in Moscow have done an excellent job in developing the overall strategy, but we have to be able to execute the strategy properly."

"I'm as prepared as possible, but don't you expect the

Panzer Tank will stop Randall and his taskforce?"

"We can't be absolutely certain of that. We must be prepared for every possibility."

"Like I just told you, if Randall and his taskforce somehow get here, I won't allow them to shut us down like they've done in the previous situations. We have a strong force here."

"Don't be overconfident. We had a strong force in the other places too."

"Our defenses will kick in hard. Some are well positioned in the woods in front of the structure. Some are well positioned inside. I'm confident at least some of them will stop Randall and his taskforce in their tracks."

"And you're sure they're all in position now?" Ivan asked.

"Of course I'm sure," Taras said. "They've all been in their final positions for several minutes now. They're all well trained and I'm sure they'll stop Randall and his group from succeeding. If the tank doesn't stop them, I always prepare for the worse-case scenario, and I always have alternatives as backup plans as an extra precaution. It never hurts to have a lot of safeguards. I'll make certain we don't give Randall any chance to succeed."

"That all sounds good. Let's hope your plan and all your backup plans for this situation aren't needed. Let's hope the tank can do its job and eliminate Randall and his whole damned taskforce completely."

"If the tank doesn't stop them, we have a great ambush strategy, and we'll execute it with precision. We even have various options for how we execute depending on the exact way Randall and his group react to our initial wave of fire."

After a brief hesitation, Ivan said, "Okay, it sounds like you're as well prepared as you can possibly be."

"We are indeed."

"It's always best to not count completely on everything going right," Ivan said slowly, "but hopefully it will. I'm still betting the tank will do its job and eliminate Randall and his whole damned taskforce."

There was a brief silence.

"The tank will likely take care of things," Taras said slowly. "However, I'm fully prepared to stop Randall and his whole damned taskforce."

"Don't be overconfident," Ivan said.

Taras grunted. "I'm not, and I'll stay prepared just in case."

"Good," Ivan said. "I'll count on that." He disconnected.

Chapter 59

Colt, with his remaining group of warriors moved north along the dirt road covered with overhanging limbs of thick foliage.

Five warriors walked on each side of the road and stayed along the edge of the trees.

Everyone maintained a separation of ten yards and kept their rifles pointed forward at a 45-degree angle.

Mack's voice rang in Colt's earpiece. "I hear some helicopters. They're coming this way."

Colt spoke into his tactical microphone. "I hear them too and they're getting real close. I hope it's the ones with the Hellfire missiles. We don't want to fight a tank out here in the woods without the proper tools."

Linda gave a short laugh. "Yeah, we welcome helicopters with tank killer missiles."

As the noise in the air got louder, everyone looked up.

Through a large gap in the overhanging limbs, Colt saw the classic shapes of the two AH-64 Apache Helicopters high above them. He raised his right fist and moved it up and down.

Linda did the same thing and said into her tactical microphone, "Doesn't hurt anything to cheer them on."

*****

"Have you acquired the target?" the first Apache pilot asked into his tactical communications unit as he reduced his speed to 40 miles per hour and his altitude to 1000 feet.

The two helicopters flew side by side with a separation of about 100 yards.

"Yep, I'm locked in on the target and I also see it visually," the other helicopter pilot replied, "I'm ready to fire on your signal."

"I want to get within about a mile before we let the missiles go," the first pilot said. "I want to see what I'm shooting at if I can. I've always been a little funny that way."

"Okay with me."

Within a few seconds, the first pilot said, "Okay I see the tank on a large float and about 50 yards from the shore."

"Same here."

In another second, the first pilot said, "Let 'em fly."

A missile with a trailing stream of smoke shot out from a side of each of the attack helicopters.

*****

Colt heard a loud explosion. Due to his extensive and varied experience in Delta Force, he recognized the noise as two different explosions that were almost simultaneous.

"Sounds like each chopper released a missile," Colt said into his tactical microphone. "They should have taken out the tank. We'll find out real soon if they did."

"Copy," Mack replied.

The other warriors responded in a similar way.

Colt heard loud helicopter sounds again and then they quickly faded into the distance.

Within a few more seconds, Colt waved everyone forward.

They moved north for several minutes.

"Thought I heard something," Linda said into her tactical microphone. "We might have some company."

Everyone took cover and waited.

Colt's internal alarms were screaming. His instinct told him danger was present, but where were the assassins?

Everyone continued to scan the area.

After five minutes of scanning, no one saw any of the enemy.

Colt stayed on high alert and gestured for everyone to move forward. "We can't stop forever. Keep your separation of about ten yards and let's keep going."

Colt saw some movement ahead. Something protruded from behind a large trunk. It was a rifle barrel.

"Down!" Colt yelled as bullets sprayed the area around him. He had followed his own command, and he rolled toward the nearest large tree as more shots rang out, showering him with splinters from the trunk.

All the other taskforce members also rolled behind cover.

The shooting stopped as suddenly as it had begun.

"Everyone okay?" Colt asked into his tactical communications unit.

The rest of the taskforce answered in the affirmative.

Colt felt a measure of relief. Staying as flat against the tree trunk as possible, he peered around it and continued to scan the area in the direction the shots had come from.

He detected no movement, but surely the enemy was still out there.

"We'll wait a few more minutes," Colt said into his tactical microphone. "If we don't have any activity, we'll stay on full alert and carefully move forward again. They might have moved to another location."

Colt fished his secure satellite phone from a pocket and pushed a button. He heard Grant answer.

"What's your status?" Grant asked.

Colt explained.

"And no casualties yet, right?"

"Right," Colt said. "We're damned good and we've been a little bit lucky too."

"That's a good combination. I hope things keep going well. We're depending on your mission being successful," Grant replied. "Hold on a minute."

Colt waited. He could faintly hear another conversation at Grant's end of the line.

In a few more seconds, Colt clearly heard Grant's voice again.

"That was Charles. He always calls on a different line than the one I use to talk to you, and I always answer on a different phone," Grant said. "He told me he had just received confirmation from the Navy that what's left of the tank is at the bottom of the body of water it was on."

"We only heard one set of explosions," Colt said. "We figured they did the job."

"The pilots reported they circled a couple of times until the tank and its carrier had sunk completely. Guess it doesn't take long for all that weight to disappear below the surface of the water."

Colt gave a short laugh and said, "Yeah."

"Due to the infrared sensors on several of our satellites, we have your position pinpointed.

Making no comment, Colt waited for Grant to continue.

"You're a little less than a mile away from the next missile structure and you're two miles away from Titov's headquarters building."

"We'll stay on high alert," Colt said. "It's likely we're going to encounter a lot of resistance before we go much further. They'll probably be using some heavy weapons."

"I think you're right and I hope you can continue without taking on some casualties."

"We're a good fighting force and I think we can handle whatever they end up throwing at us."

"Well, anyway, you shouldn't have to worry about a tank," Grant said. "Good luck on the rest of your mission."

"Thanks. We'll stay in touch."

Colt heard Grant disconnect.

After waiting another minute, Colt stepped out from behind the tree. No one fired at him.

He scanned the area again and detected no threats, so he waved everyone forward.

The ten remaining members of the taskforce continued to move north with everyone staying evenly divided, five warriors were on each side of the road.

As they moved north another half mile, Colt was surprised they had encountered no additional resistance, but he had just heard an ominous noise. It sounded like a tank. He called a halt and told everyone to take cover. He moved quickly behind a large tree trunk.

Colt heard the noise coming closer and he also heard Mack's voice in his earpiece.

"That sounds like a tank," Mack said. "It's either that or some other heavy piece of equipment."

The sound drew closer. It was now a clear heavy rumble.

"It's definitely a tank," Colt said into his tactical microphone. "You never forget that sound once you've fought a few of them. And I had that experience many times with Delta Force." He fished his secure satellite phone from a pocket. "I'll call Grant and request that the helicopters come back. We need their help before it's too late. We don't have any weapons among us we can use to fight any heavily armored vehicle, especially tanks."

Colt heard Linda's voice in his earpiece. "Let's hope they don't start dropping large shells on us. We have a lot of good equipment, but none of us brought along any shovels to dig foxholes."

"Start looking for any ditches or any other low areas you can get in," Colt said into his tactical microphone. "If you can't find a ditch, any type of low area will be better than high ground."

"Roger, we're looking for the lowest area we can find," Mack replied.

Colt narrowed his eyes as he pushed a button on his phone.

Chapter 60

Ivan sat with Sergei at the large table in the main conference room in his headquarters. They both studied the various wall-mounted monitors around the room.

Ivan stared at Sergei through narrowed eyes. “Things aren’t working out very well at the moment. Losing the tank was a big setback.”

Sergei clinched both fists, pursed his lips, and looked straight down at the table.

“I keep telling you Randall is tough to eliminate.” Ivan shook his head slowly. “And it now appears he and his whole damned taskforce will be even tougher to eliminate.”

A brief silence ensued.

Sergei looked up and quickly scanned the numerous monitors along the walls.

“We lost the tank, but we still have a lot of resistance in place,” Sergei said. “If we hurry, we can still get the remaining missile launched.”

"Maybe we'll have some better luck going forward."

"We have a tremendous amount of skilled warriors remaining. With any good luck at all we should still be able to stop Randall."

Ivan grunted and leaned forward. "It's too damned bad we lost the tank. That would have been a big help."

Sergei nodded. "I agree, but we still have a lot of firepower left. We have teams outside the missile structure and inside. I just talked with both team leaders a few minutes ago. They each have their ambush set up."

Ivan glanced at his watch. "A lot can happen within a few minutes in an active war zone." He narrowed his eyes and jutted out his chin. "And that's exactly what we have here, an active war zone."

Sergei didn't comment.

Ivan looked at Sergei and said, "You call Dmitri again and get an update on his readiness to hack into the Federal Reserve System with the quantum computer. I'll call Taras and make sure he's fully ready to cope with Randall and his taskforce."

"You just finished checking all that out with him. Why do you need to do that again?"

"Like I just mentioned, we're in an active war zone. It won't hurt anything to check again, just in case."

Sergei nodded slowly and then reached for his phone.

Ivan also grabbed his phone.

Both men punched a button.

Ivan heard Taras answer immediately.

"Is everything still ready for action?" Ivan asked.

"Not a damned thing has changed," Taras replied sharply. "Are you concerned about something in particular?"

"I'm concerned about everything. I wanted to check with you again and make sure we're as ready as we can be."

"You're looking for reassurance?"

Ivan hesitated a moment and then said, "Basically yes."

"We're as ready as we can be."

"Any update on the progress for getting the missile ready to launch?" Ivan asked.

"Dmitri and Pavel both emphasized we need to make sure it's going to function properly and hit the target once it's launched," Taras said. "They told me we're close, but it's going to take a few more minutes."

"Exactly how many minutes are you talking about?" Ivan asked.

Taras hesitated and his voice echoed some concern. "Is Randall closing in on us?"

"Damned right he is." Ivan looked at a monitor showing infrared images. "Looks like he and his whole taskforce are stopped at the moment, but they're less than a mile from you."

"We're as ready as we're ever going to be," Taras said in a calmer voice. "Let them come. We'll stop them and get the missile launched."

Ivan didn't comment.

"Are you still there?" Taras asked.

"Yeah, I'm thinking."

"I'll give you my utmost assurance we're ready for Randall and his whole taskforce."

"Okay I'm okay for now," Ivan said slowly, "we'll stay in close touch. Keep me posted on any changes."

"Will do."

Ivan disconnected and looked at Sergei who had finished his latest phone conversation with Dmitri.

"Well?" Ivan asked.

"Dmitri told me they have everything ready with all the computers to start their hacking attempt. He and Pavel have both rechecked things and are waiting for our command."

Ivan narrowed his eyes and started to say something

when his phone rang. He saw it was Lev calling and he answered.

"Got an update for you," Lev said with extra vigor. "We have another tank and it's closing in on Randall's position."

"How did that happen?"

"My bosses used a different method to get it over to your island. They used a ferry that had a top and could carry heavy loads. It's one that's been used several times before so it shouldn't have attracted any attention from all the people who're studying the satellite images."

"The images would still show the tank being driven onto the ferry."

"You may have forgotten, but the ferry landing on both sides of the water is covered by overhanging limbs. The forest grows all the way down to the water in that area."

"Very very good," Ivan said. He laughed. "It's great we still have a tank in this fight."

"Yes, and it should be well on its way toward Randall's position."

Chapter 61

Colt held his phone to his right ear which didn't have the earpiece for his tactical communications system. He heard Grant answer.

"I can't explain it," Colt said. "But there's a tank coming in our direction. The noise is getting louder by the minute. It must be on the road. It can't maneuver through all the trees."

"Are you sure it's a tank?"

"Positive. It has a distinctive sound that I recognize easily. I was in a lot of tank battles when I was in Delta Force."

"I'll call you back and ask you more questions later. I'll get in touch with Charles immediately and see if we can get the Apache helicopters back out there. He has a direct connection to the Navy."

Colt heard Grant disconnect and then spoke into his tactical communications microphone, "I've talked to Grant.

He's trying to get the helicopters back out here. Stay in the best cover you can find and I'll keep you posted."

"If we have to fight the damned tank, do you have any suggestions?" Mack asked.

"They'll probably have a guy up on top looking for us," Colt said. "We could shoot him, but that would give away our positions. Also, we don't want to be close enough to do that. We want to stay as far away as we can."

"So, we won't try to disable the tank by concentrating fire on the treads?" Mack asked.

Colt grunted. "No, we don't have any of the right weapons for that. Plus, again, if we start shooting, it will give away our positions, and the tank will start lobbing highly explosive shells in our direction. If it gets much closer we might consider pulling back deeper into the woods. I'll keep everyone posted. Stay tuned."

"Roger," came multiple replies.

Feeling a little more anxious than usual, Colt waited for Grant to call back.

There was no way they could fight a tank without the proper weapons, Colt thought. Having a bazooka or some type of handheld rocket launcher with the right type of shells would be invaluable, but that was not the case. No one had anticipated having to fight a tank.

Colt felt his phone, which he was still holding in his right hand, vibrate. He answered immediately.

"The AH-64 Apache Helicopters are on their way," Grant said. "Each of them still has a tank killer missile mounted. It's lucky the pilots were still in them and doing some post-flight checks on things. They should be in your area within another ten minutes."

"Great."

"I was advised to tell you to move well away from the road and go south as fast as you can. You don't want to be too close to the explosions."

"Roger," Colt said. "I'll give the order immediately.

We'll concentrate on getting deeper into the woods. That tank can move pretty quickly on the road, but it will probably slow down a little for the guy who's probably up on top to look for us."

"Good luck and call me back immediately if the helicopters do their job again and this second tank is eliminated. Hopefully this is the last one."

"I'll keep in touch."

Colt heard Grant disconnect and he immediately put his phone back in his pocket while he spoke into his tactical communications unit, "The helicopters should be back here in about ten minutes. We'll all stay on the side of the road we're currently on and pull back about a half mile deeper into the woods. After you get deep enough into the woods, move to the south."

"Roger," came multiple replies.

Chapter 62

Ivan looked at his ringing phone. The caller ID only showed a number, and he didn't recognize that number. He hesitated.

Sergei gestured toward the phone. "It might have something to do with the tank. It might even be the tank commander."

"It could also be a trick," Ivan said. "The Americans might have found out how to contact us. It might even be Randall."

"I doubt its Randall. He's probably scrambling around to try to avoid the tank."

Ivan narrowed his eyes and didn't comment.

Sergei gestured toward the phone again. "I think you should go ahead and answer it. I don't think we have anything to lose."

Ivan reached for the phone and answered.

"I'm in command of the tank that's passing by your headquarters. Lev Petrov told me to coordinate with you," the tank commander said. "Lev told me you're receiving the infrared images from the satellites, and you can give me the exact location of the enemy force."

"Your tank gives off heat too and I can see you're exactly two and a half miles from the enemy group."

"Got it," the tank commander said.

"You'll pass another structure that's a mile from you. We have a lot of forces in the woods around it so don't do any firing until you've gone at least two more miles. I'll let you know when you get to the enemy force."

"Understood," the tank commander replied.

"How many shells do you have?"

"Twelve," the tank commander said. "We managed to cram a few extra into this tank."

Ivan narrowed his eyes. "That should be enough to do a lot of damage to Randall, maybe even eliminate them completely."

"I'll disconnect now and concentrate on eliminating Randall and his taskforce," the tank commander said. "I need to concentrate. I'll call you back if I have any more questions."

"Good luck," Ivan said. "You can do some real damage to Randall's efforts."

"Roger."

Ivan heard the tank commander disconnect and he drummed his fingers on the table as he turned toward Sergei.

"The tank commander told me his tank has twelve shells, and I think that can do a lot of damage to Randall and his taskforce," Ivan said.

"That's a lot. Is that how many a Panzer Tank carries normally?"

"I didn't ask."

Sergei leaned toward Ivan. "Did you find out what type of shells they are and how powerful they're supposed to be?"

"The tank commander didn't say and again I didn't ask

him," Ivan said. "I'm sure they're powerful enough to do the job."

Sergei pursed his lips and nodded slowly.

There was a brief silence.

"We'll find out real soon how effective the tank is," Ivan said. "At the very least, Randall's taskforce should should suffer a few causalities this time. I don't think they'll have enough cover to avoid a lot of serious injuries to a lot of people."

Sergei continued to nod.

Chapter 63

Colt found a circular hollow about twenty feet deep and ten yards in diameter that was about 100 yards from the road. It afforded a relatively clear view of the road, and the western bank of the hollow had a gradual slope. He decided to stop there and try to observe what the tank would be doing.

"I'm going to stop about a hundred yards from the road and keep an eye on what the tank is doing. That could turn out to be a big help to all of us," Colt said into his tactical microphone. "Linda you join me. Everyone else follow the previous plan."

"That's going to be dangerous," Mack replied. "You're going to be taking a big risk."

"We have a good hollow to stop in. It's about twenty feet deep and it will offer some good protection from anything but a direct hit," Colt said. "While we're waiting for the helicopters to show up, it's good to know where the tank is located and what it's doing at that exact moment."

"Can't Grant keep you posted on that by having you on the phone while he's looking at the infrared images?" Mack asked.

"That would involve a few seconds delay. What I'll be doing will be a lot better for us."

"I hear you," Mack said. "Good luck."

Linda hurried forward and crawled into the hollow with Colt. They stayed about three yards apart and lay as flat on the ground as they could, close to the top of the gradual slope. They wanted to be close enough to talk as things developed, but still maintain a little distance.

They both had an excellent view of about a thirty-yard stretch of road, and they both could quickly roll down further into the hollow if they needed to. They were perfectly set up for observation, and they maintained some measure of protection from being down a ways in the hollow.

Soon after he and Linda got settled in their positions, Colt heard the tank sounds get louder. He figured it was coming toward them at its maximum speed. He wasn't sure exactly how fast a Panzer Tank could go, but apparently it was at least thirty miles per hour.

"It surely sounds like it's getting close," Linda said, "but I don't see it yet."

"I think you'll see it real soon. Keep watching. I just hope it doesn't stop when it gets even with us," Colt replied. "That would mean they're getting information from Ivan Titov who's probably watching the infrared images coming from the satellites."

"Titov probably won't have any trouble figuring things out when he sees two heat images the size of human figures well away from the others." Linda said while looking at Colt. "He'll guess one of them has to be you."

In less than a minute, Colt saw the tank stop on the road directly in front of his and Linda's position. He saw the turret with the long barrel turning toward him.

"Roll to the bottom," Colt said.

He and Linda both responded quickly just before two

trees close together and a little to the right and behind the hollow both exploded into splinters.

Colt noted all the splinters flew over them. None fell into the hollow. The ground in the low area where they were was completely undisturbed.

"Looks like you're right. They figured it out," Colt said. "The tank commander is probably talking to Titov now and trying to get the coordinates of our position a little more precise."

"Do you think we should move?" Linda asked.

"I think we'll be safer to stay put right here at the bottom and keep our heads down," Colt replied. "I don't know how accurately a Panzer Tank can lob shells. We'll be okay if they don't drop a shell right on top of us."

"Roger."

Colt fought off a temptation to crawl up to the top of the slope and look at the tank. However, he decided to follow his own advice.

"You guys okay?" Mack asked.

"So far," Colt said. "I hope those helicopters can get here before the tank gets many more shots at us."

"Six of us are heading toward the road," Mack said. "That should give Titov something to think about as he's looking at the infrared images. Maybe it will create enough of a diversion to buy a little more time for the helicopters to do their job."

"How far away from the road are you?" Colt asked.

"Still about a half mile, but we're moving fast," Mack said. "We should definitely attract some attention. Titov can't know for sure we haven't been able to get some anti-tank weapons. He's probably letting the tank commander know about us right now."

"Thanks," Colt replied. "Anything besides Linda and me that can hold their attention for a minute or so could be a big help."

"The least we can do." Mack hesitated for a moment.

"We all have to help each other any way we can."

"Appreciated," Colt said as he felt the phone vibrate in his pocket. He answered and immediately heard Grant's voice.

"Charles just called and told me the helicopters should be making their stretch run any moment," Grant said. "You shouldn't have long to wait. I'll hang up and let you take care of business."

Colt heard Grant disconnect and he immediately spoke into his tactical communications microphone. "The helicopters should be here any moment. Take the best cover you can get. We're about to hear a couple of big explosions and this time they're going to be a lot closer than before."

"Roger," came multiple replies.

Colt and Linda pressed the ground at the bottom of the hollow as hard as they could.

The noise from the helicopters became increasing louder than the sound from the tank. Colt figured the explosions he was expecting were imminent.

*****

"Do you have the tank lined up on TADS?" The first helicopter pilot asked into his tactical communications unit as he reduced speed to 60 miles per hour and flew directly above the dirt road as instructed. He maintained a position of about ten yards from the left side of the road.

"Yes I do, we're within seven miles now," the second helicopter pilot replied as he flew about thirty yards to the right of the other helicopter. "I'm getting a clear signal on the target and I'm locked on it."

"Good," the first pilot said. "I have a visual on the tank now and I'm also locked in on the target."

“I have a visual on it too and everything is green on TADS,” the second pilot replied.

“Good,” the first pilot said quickly. “Let ‘em rip, goodbye tank.”

A missile with a stream of smoke behind it shot out from each helicopter.

*****

As soon as Colt heard the explosions, he and Linda crawled back up the slope to the top of the hollow.

“That’s just what I wanted to see,” Colt said, “a burning heap of twisted steel.”

Several muffled explosions went off inside the tank.

“If anyone survived the tank killer missile hits, there’s no way they’re alive now,” Linda said.

Colt nodded. “I don’t know how many shells they had inside the tank, but several have exploded.”

After waiting about a minute and hearing a few more explosions, Colt spoke into his tactical microphone, “Let’s go about 100 yards north of the tank and regroup into our original formation. I would advise staying well away from the tank as you go by it. There could be some more explosions.”

“Roger,” came multiple replies.

Colt and Linda stayed about 100 yards off the road and went north of the demolished and still smoking tank. They waited for the other members of their team to join them.

In about fifteen minutes, the eight other agents on the remaining taskforce joined Colt and Linda. In a few more seconds, they were all moving north again in their tactical formation.

Chapter 64

In the Kremlin, Lev sat in his well-padded chair at the large mahogany desk in his office and studied the images on one of the wall-mounted monitors. He drummed the fingers of his right hand on his desk for a few seconds before he looked at Yuri, who was sitting in front of him.

"It's probably time to compare notes with Ivan again," Lev said. "Do you want to call him or do you want me to?"

Yuri grunted. "Let's talk things over for a few minutes and then we'll decide on that."

"Do you have some specifics in mind you want us to agree on?"

"Yeah," Yuri said, "and we better make damned sure we're fully in agreement before we talk about them to Ivan and Sergei."

"Ivan and Sergei are multi-billionaires, and they've been getting a lot of help from China," Lev said slowly. His eyes flashed. "We thought they could pull off Project

Neptune with very limited help from the Kremlin. It looks like we were wrong."

"You think Randall and his taskforce are going to succeed in shutting everything down where Ivan had things set up for the attack on the United States?"

Lev nodded slowly. "That's the way it looks right now. We've lost the two warehouses and the first missile structure. And now we've lost both the tanks. Also, it looks like Ivan might have withdrawn all his assassins who were outside the second missile structure."

"Damn," Yuri said. "We need to ask him about that when we call."

"I hope he had a good reason." Lev put both his palms flat on his desk and leaned toward Yuri. "Since the tank had a lot of high-explosive shells, maybe he thought it would be able to completely eliminate Randall and his whole damned taskforce."

"It probably would have been good to leave his assassins out there in the woods to mop up."

Lev pursed his lips. "Maybe he thought they might get targeted by the tank. When you're going by the infrared images from the satellites, it would be easy for somebody to get a little confused, especially if Randall's group and our assassins were spread out all over the area."

"Are you going to call right now?" Yuri leaned forward. "We might not have much more time to keep Randall away from our only remaining Poseidon Missile. I think Ivan had security devices installed in all his structures. That will help a lot in being able to repel Randall when he gets inside this last missile structure."

Lev nodded slowly and then said, "None of that has stopped Randall so far, but maybe it will stop him this next time." He picked up his phone and punched in a number.

*****

In the main conference room in his headquarters in the archipelago, Ivan glanced at Sergei as he reached for his ringing phone.

"It's either Lev or Yuri," Ivan said. He leaned forward and answered.

"Have you been watching the activity?" Ivan asked.

"I saw our tank has been destroyed and I know you pulled your assassins back from in the woods."

"I didn't want them mistakenly targeted by the tank."

"Understood."

"We could really use support from some attack helicopters."

"I've already made it clear my bosses won't provide any Military attack helicopters," Lev said.

"That's too bad," Ivan replied. "We can't allow Randall to stop us again. We only have one missile left and we must launch it this time."

"Remember, my bosses in the Kremlin want to be able to deny they had any part in this attempt to bring down the United States. They don't want a world war. The United States used some of their Military attack helicopters because they knew they were being directly threatened by the Poseidon Missiles."

"Don't forget we're being threatened too. Randall and his taskforce are over here on our soil."

"My bosses keep reminding me they're not on Russian soil and they're not threatening the Kremlin," Lev said. "Randall and his taskforce are not threatening Russia, Moscow, or the Kremlin. They're trying to eliminate a threat to the United States that you and Sergei are behind."

"So, you're still going to blame everything on us?"

"The United States knows who you are and what

you're doing. They found all that out when you were in Jamaica."

"They found out you were behind this too."

"We still have deniability. Do I have to explain all that to you again?"

There was a brief silence.

"Well at least I have Taras and a lot of other talented assassins to meet Randall and his taskforce when they enter our last missile structure," Ivan said. "Maybe we'll be able to stop them this time."

"You definitely have a chance. Good luck."

Ivan heard Lev disconnect and then looked at Sergei.

"Well, you listened to my side of the conversation," Ivan said. "Do you have any questions?"

Sergei shrugged. "I think everything is clear. I didn't expect anything different. I hope Taras and the assassins around him can come through for us this time."

Ivan said, "If they don't, we might consider getting the hell out of here and going back to Moscow. We both still have several nice homes there."

Sergei gave a vigorous nod.

Chapter 65

After traveling through the woods for several minutes, Colt approached the next structure. He spoke into his tactical communications unit, "We'll use the same plan as we used in the last missile structure to check this one out."

"Roger," came multiple replies.

Colt moved toward the back entrance and waved everyone forward. The others in his team of ten followed in single file and stayed about five yards apart.

Within a few more seconds, Colt turned the knob on the door at the back of the structure.

The door was locked.

Mack eased up beside Colt and removed a small kit from a vest pocket. He used a pick and the ten warriors eased cautiously through the doorway and looked for cover inside the warehouse.

They were in an empty room.

Other than a red door on the wall straight ahead, a concrete floor and bare walls dominated their view.

The ceiling was flat and bare. It was an off-white color. Colt saw no evidence of any cameras on the walls or the ceiling.

Colt, Linda and Mack moved up beside the red door.

Before he opened the door, Colt spoke into his tactical microphone, "We're probably going to encounter one hell of a lot of opposition when we get close to the missile area or the computer area, especially if we're getting close to both of them. Be ready for action."

"Roger," came multiple replies.

Colt eased the door open and peered into the next area.

It was a large room with a lot of metal crates and various pieces of large equipment scattered about.

Colt and Linda led the way as everyone spread out in the wide room and moved forward slowly. Colt estimated the room was about thirty yards wide and fifty yards long.

Everyone kept their rifles pointed forward and ready to use.

When bullets ricocheted of a large forklift a few yards in front of them, Colt and Linda dropped and pressed flat against the concrete floor. They were about five yards apart.

More bullets were fired and bounced off the floor a few yards to the left of Colt.

After the flurry of bullets stopped, Colt stayed as low as he could and crawled over to Linda's position behind a large metal crate, which was a cube about eight feet on all sides.

"You see anyone?" Colt asked.

"Not yet," Linda said, "but I think we should stay in good cover and keep looking for a while."

Colt nodded and spoke into his tactical microphone, giving everyone on the taskforce the same advice.

While peering around the corner of the crate he was behind, Colt saw a figure emerge from behind a piece of equipment about twenty yards away and then dart immediately behind another piece of equipment.

"Did you see him?" Linda asked.

"Yeah," Colt said. "He'll probably keep coming this way. Don't shoot him immediately. We can use a prisoner to get some information."

Linda glanced at Colt and nodded.

Colt kept a keen watch and waited patiently for the assassin to appear again as he and Linda remained hidden.

The assassin appeared again and darted quickly behind the next piece of equipment as he continued toward Colt's and Linda's position.

When the assassin appeared again, Colt waited a few seconds for him to get closer and then stepped out from behind the crate.

Colt pointed his SIG 556 at the muscular assassin.

"Drop the rifle or you die immediately," Colt said. He kept his SIG 556 trained on the assassin.

The assassin dropped his AK-74 and grinned. "Okay Randall, I know you don't have a reputation for shooting defenseless people."

"How do you know who I am?" Colt asked.

The assassin smirked. "I'm well briefed about you, and your photograph has been widely distributed."

"You know my name. Who are you?" Colt asked.

"Taras Popov, you've probably heard of me."

Colt narrowed his eyes. "I don't think so. Are you a new addition to the fighting force here?"

Taras looked disappointed and didn't comment.

Linda came up closer to Colt.

Staring hard at Taras, Colt said, "Okay Popov, lose the pistol."

Taras stood motionless. He looked directly at Colt and flashed another grin. "I suspect you're afraid to fight me like a real tough guy would."

"Do you mean hand-to-hand?" Colt asked.

Taras continued to grin. "That would seem fair to me."

"Why would I want to do that?"

"To prove you're the better man, of course."

"I don't have any interest in proving that."

Taras gave a slight shrug. "I never thought you'd be too chicken." He gestured toward Linda. "You even have her backing you up."

"You've stalled long enough. Lose the pistol now." Colt gestured with his SIG 556 and essentially kept it trained on Taras's chest.

Taras continued to stand still.

"I'll shoot him if you won't," Linda said. "We can't afford to spend any more time here." She glanced at Colt. "Well?"

"Give me a few more seconds," Colt said. He turned fully toward Taras. "I'm asking you just one more time to drop your pistol on the floor. If you don't do it now I'll have to kill you." He paused. "You're being stupid to bring that on yourself."

Taras flashed an impish grin. "If you do that then that would be murder and you don't have a reputation for murdering people."

"I don't have Colt's reputation," Linda said. "I'll shoot you any time I get ready. And I'm ready now." She pointed her SIG 556 at Taras's chest.

Multiple gunshots rang out to Colt's right. Some were loud and some were soft pops. It was clear both sides were shooting. Colt was glad to hear more soft pops than loud bangs.

Colt watched Taras's impish grin expand. The hate seemed to burn bright in his eyes.

More gunshots erupted, again a mixture of loud bangs and soft pops.

"I have a lot of support in here," Taras said. "Everyone with me is a great warrior. We'll soon overwhelm you."

Colt and Linda each kept their SIG 556 pointed at Taras as he continued to grin.

A brief silence ensued.

With lightning speed, Taras moved his right hand

toward his pistol.

Colt and Linda both fired.

Taras's pistol tumbled to the concrete floor along with him.

The high-powered bullets tore a hole in his chest. He obviously wasn't wearing any bulletproof clothing.

Avoiding the growing pool of blood, Colt walked over and felt for a pulse. There was none.

"He must have thought we were distracted by all the shooting," Colt said. He glanced at Linda. "I guess he figured that would be his best chance to catch us off guard."

Linda nodded. "Lucky for us, his thinking turned out to be wrong, dead wrong."

Colt grunted. "I guess we could say that's an accurate statement. In fact, it's dead accurate."

Linda gave a thumbs-up along with a slight grin.

While continuing to scan the area around them, Colt saw Mack approaching their position.

"We eliminated a lot of others over our way," Mack said as he got close. He stared at Taras on the floor for a moment. "I think we have them all cleared out there must have been around thirty assassins over our way. I didn't stick around for an exact count. Our guys are still searching the area just in case. We don't want to leave any stone unturned, as the saying goes."

In another few seconds, Colt heard an 'all clear' message in his earpiece.

"Good job," Colt said, looking at Mack.

Mack nodded and raised his right fist in the air.

Colt spoke into his tactical microphone, "Everyone move back toward the left side of the room where Mack, Linda, and I are positioned. Stay alert in case you missed someone. When you get here we'll move forward again."

In less than a minute, seven more warriors kept good separation and gathered in the area around Colt.

"Let's keep moving, there's probably another red door in front of us. We must find the missile as soon as possible," Colt said quickly. "We might not have much time left."

The ten warriors moved forward and quickly found the expected red door on the far wall in front of them. It was unlocked.

Colt stood to the side of the door and eased it open.

Everyone moved forward. The sight through the doorway was startling.

Chapter 66

Ivan sat with Sergei at the large table in the main conference room in his headquarters. They both studied the large group of wall-mounted monitors.

"Well, we've lost almost all of our assassins," Ivan said, "and it looks like we're about to lose the missile." He pointed to one of the monitors.

Sergei nodded as he looked directly at Ivan. "Do you think it's time to leave?"

"We still have our moles in the United States Government, and they all have close connections to China. They can still keep things moving on bringing down the United States and they can keep things moving with China if the Kremlin wants to continue that relationship," Ivan said. "You and I can still manage a lot of that from Moscow."

"Do you think the Kremlin will continue to want to stay closely connected with China?"

"I'm not sure." Ivan wrinkled his brow. "But we can think about all that later."

Sergei leaned forward. "So, you're ready to go?"

"Our boat is ready and waiting to take us back to the mainland and our private plane is waiting at the airport. There's no reason now for us to stay here and be killed or captured."

Sergei nodded.

Ivan narrowed his eyes and stood. "I don't think we should wait around any longer." He pointed to some of the images from cameras mounted inside the second missile structure. They showed Colt Randall and his taskforce at the last red door and getting ready to charge into the missile room.

"Let's get Pavel and Dmitri back over here to go with us," Sergei said. "I'm sure the Kremlin and China are both developing more quantum computers and more supercomputers. Our two technical experts will be a big help to us in the future."

"Go ahead and call them. Tell them to hurry and to meet us at the boat."

Sergei picked up his phone and punched a digit. He gave Pavel the instructions and then looked at Ivan. "They're leaving now. They know Randall is in the building and they're close to an emergency exit."

Ivan gave a thumbs-up.

"We can be sure the Kremlin is producing more Poseidon Missiles, and we can also be sure the Chinese will continue to help with that effort," Sergei said as he and Ivan rushed toward the closest emergency exit. "Given time, we can figure out a better way to launch a successful attack on the United States in the future."

"We can only do that if we get the hell out of here and not get killed or captured," Ivan said. He opened the door and rushed down some concrete steps to an underground tunnel.

Sergei followed.

*****

Colt again had the same odd feeling as before, something like having a sudden encounter with a large monster. He quickly shook off the feeling and concentrated on the situation.

Another one of the huge Poseidon Missiles loomed before him. It was on top of the same type of mobile launcher as the other one was.

Like the other missile, the nose cone of the 80-foot-long and 8-foot-wide cylinder was like that of a large jet, but it was much more menacing.

A large opening in the wall in front of the mobile launcher revealed the dirt road leading back to the launch site. The metal door was open."

"We got here just in time," Colt said into his tactical microphone. "They're ready to move the missile to the launch site."

"Let's get busy," Mack replied.

Colt and Linda led the team through the doorway and toward the nearest cover. Which was a horizontal row formed by a lot of large metal crates.

Everyone spread out along the row of crates.

Linda and Mack stayed with Colt at the left end of the row.

Colt peered around the corner of the crate he was behind. But he pulled back quickly when several bursts of high caliber bullets rattled off the row of metal crates in multiple places.

"They must not have been expecting us to arrive this quickly," Mack said. "They're a little late in firing."

"I've seen the cameras in the ceiling and I'm sure Ivan Titov and Sergei Nikitin have been watching us," Colt replied. "They must have lost their communication somehow with their team over here."

"They probably evacuated like they did in Jamaica." Linda glanced at Colt. "What else would you expect?"

Colt pursed his lips and gave a quick nod just as several more bursts of high caliber bullets ricocheted in all directions off the metal crates and the concrete floor.

All the warriors in the taskforce hugged the concrete floor and stayed as flat as possible.

When the barrage of bullets stopped, Colt again peered around the corner of the crate he was behind.

He saw several enemy assassins about twenty yards away and coming toward him.

"Get ready for action. Some of the enemy assassins are coming directly toward us," Colt spoke into his tactical microphone as he leaned out from the corner of the crate and started firing, a series of soft pops came from his SIG 556 due to his sound suppression device.

The assassins coming toward him all toppled limply to the floor.

Colt heard a lot of other soft pops coming from his right before he stepped out from behind the crate and raced forward toward the next cover, which was the mobile launcher.

Mack and Linda followed Colt.

The three of them kept their rifles pointed forward at a 45-degree angle as they charged toward the mobile launcher. Each of them kept a finger tight on the trigger and was prepared to fire within a fraction of a second.

Colt charged toward the left side of the mobile launcher. Linda and Mack followed him.

The rest of the warriors in the taskforce charged toward the right side.

No more assassins were found.

Colt spoke into his tactical communications microphone, "Spread out and stay alert. We don't want to get hit by a surprise attack."

"Roger," came multiple replies.

After a few more minutes of looking around and finding no more threats, Colt glanced at Linda and Mack. "I think things are all clear. It looks like we've cleaned them out."

Linda and Mack both nodded.

Colt looked directly at Linda. "I'm sure you're right that Titov and Nikitin have evacuated, but we'll check the headquarters building anyway." He left four men to secure the structure with the missile and the quantum computer before he waved his remaining group forward.

After getting to Titov's headquarters building, Colt had three men surround it and keep watch while he, Linda, and Mack went inside.

Finding the building empty of people, as expected, Colt said, "I think we've wrapped this one up."

"We did a great job, but it's too damned bad we let Titov and Nikitin escape again," Mack said. "We should have anticipated that."

"It might not be too late," Colt said. He removed his secure satellite phone from a pocket and punched a digit. "I'll give Grant a report."

Linda and Mack both stayed on alert and continued to scan the area.

After a brief conversation, Colt looked at Linda and Mack and said, "Grant told me the President has agreed to send a large Navy force up here to do the cleanup and secure the area. They'll move the Poseidon Missiles to the appropriate military facility."

Linda and Mack both nodded.

"Grant also told me they've alerted the Finish authorities about Titov," Colt said. "They think Titov probably has his plane at the nearest airport to his island and Finland's authorities have agreed to immediately call the airport traffic control to stop him from taking off. The

Finish authorities have also agreed to send an armed detail to impound the plane."

"That's good," Mack replied. "Maybe we'll capture Titov and Nikitin this time."

Linda nodded and gave a thumbs-up.

"And another good thing," Colt said. "As soon as the Navy force gets here and is in place, we've been ordered to go home."

"Great," Linda and Mack replied in unison.

Chapter 67

Late the next day in Tampa, Grant sat at the large table in the main conference room at FBI headquarters and reviewed the current situation with the contingent from Boswic.

Colt, Linda, Harlan, Jim, and Blake sat across the table from Grant.

Grant looked at Colt and Linda. "Great job up there in the archipelago, once again you couldn't have done any better."

Colt and Linda each gave a thumbs-up.

"Ken gave me a status report, and it looks like we're in great shape," Grant said. "The Navy has completely inspected and secured the whole area. Ivan Titov, Sergei Nikitin, Pavel Werner, and Dmitri Fedorov have all been arrested and are in the custody of our Navy. The two Poseidon Missiles have been loaded onto a Navy ship and are being transported to one of our military bases."

"Well, I hope we keep Titov and his group in jail for a long time," Colt said. "If they ever get free, they're certain to get involved in another project to bring us down."

Linda nodded. "And China will probably be helping them again."

Grant leaned forward. "Whatever those two countries do now, they're without four Poseidon Missiles, two powerful quantum computers, and two powerful supercomputers we've confiscated while shutting down their threats from Jamaica and the archipelago off the west coast of Finland."

Harlan raised a fist in the air. "That's a big plus for the United States as things go forward."

Everyone else also made some type of victory gesture.

"We know for sure China is still involved in a lot of schemes to tear down our economy," Blake said. "I've completed a lot more research on that."

"And we also know for sure China is still cooperating directly with Russia on some specific things we know about, and we figure they're continuing to cooperate on a lot of other things too," Grant replied. "We must keep in mind that China and Russia have a lot of mutual interests."

Blake nodded. "It's worth mentioning they both want to try to bring us down in as many ways as they can. One of the ways is by supporting the drug trafficking into our country. They both like the cash flow they get from supporting the drug trafficking from both South America and Central America."

"The continued influx of illegal drugs into the United States will certainly help them destabilize our country," Jim said. "We need to do a lot more to eliminate that activity."

Harlan clinched a fist. "We must figure out all the details of their drug operations before it's too late. At least we've again avoided being hit by an underwater nuclear missile. We must remain vigilant on that too. They've come too close for comfort twice now."

Grant narrowed his eyes. "We know the Russians will probably build a lot more Poseidon Missiles and China will be heavily involved. We can be sure all the new models will incorporate the latest advanced technology developed by the Chinese."

There was a brief silence.

"I think the Russian leaders probably feel at a distinct disadvantage to China on several things," Blake said. "Russia probably wants to gain ground on China in as many ways as they can. They definitely don't want China to be able to take them over after they both cooperate to bring the United States down."

Grant scanned the faces around the table and then leaned forward. "Yeah, I understand the consensus at the CIA is that Russia will continue attempts to gain more international clout in any way that they can. Bringing the United States down and being able to stand up to China are probably just a few of their many goals."

Harlan grunted. "And that's the damned truth."

Blake leaned forward. "I think the Russians will try to increase their gold supply and deplete ours. Going forward they'll try to have more gold than China. We need to stay alert for that activity."

"I'll ask Ken and Charles to have Steve and Nick do more study on all that," Grant said. He looked at Blake. "If Harlan and Jim agree, I suggest you join them."

Blake gave a thumbs-up and reminded everyone that the total amount of gold that had ever been mined worldwide was around 142,000 metric tons. At 1,000 dollars per ounce, that would amount to about four and a half trillion dollars."

Everyone nodded.

Blake went on to say four and a half trillion dollars wouldn't even cover the amount of money in circulation in the United States.

"So what point are you trying to make?" Harlan asked.

"The Russians might want to deplete our gold supply mainly to disrupt us," Blake said. "The amount of our gold supply is still a primary part of what the Federal Reserve uses to promote stability." He paused. "If they somehow steal all of our gold, it won't shut us down unless we panic."

Grant narrowed his eyes and leaned forward. "We'll continue to study all the possibilities and stay alert for any advantages the Russians are trying to create for themselves." He looked at Colt. "We haven't been able to go after Lev Petrov and Yuri Werner who've mostly stayed in Moscow. They might organize a group to come after you in some way. I'm sure they want some revenge."

"I'll stay alert," Colt said. He scanned the faces around the table. "I'm sure we'll all stay alert."

Everyone nodded.

Colt figured many Russian and Chinese activities against the United States would stay active. He expected some more big global events real soon, and he was reasonably certain Boswic would be right in the middle of the activity, especially since he had recently led several major efforts that had been consistently successful.

www.ingramcontent.com/pod-product-compliance
Lightning Source LLC
LaVergne TN
LVHW052037200926
848481LV00005B/1707